The Business of Families

The Business of Families

Skills From Work
That Work At Home
Second Edition

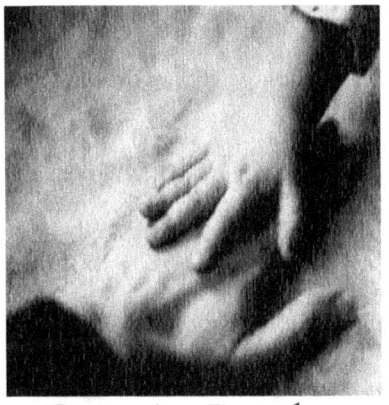

Ray A. Snyder

Foreword by Ken Blanchard

"This isn't a book about just families. It's a reference about our life at work and at home. The idea that we have to separate our work from our family is fallacy."

2005

The Business of Families

TABLE OF CONTENTS

ACKNOWLEDGMENTS

The original thought for this book comes from many of the greatest thinkers I have met or read.

Kathy, my wife, and Mary Ann, my younger daughter, have lovingly and cheerfully given me the space, insight, permission, and encouragement to write about our lives together. My parents, Ray and Louise never stopped praying for or believing in me. They, too, appear from time to time on these pages.

Ken Blanchard, my hero, provided for me what I thought was a great business opportunity that ended up defining my life's mission. Eunice Parisi-Carew and Kevin Karaffa, my sponsors at The Ken Blanchard Companies®, not only encouraged me, but also made it possible to take the time away from work and travel for this project. Kevin has run interference with our clients on my behalf as he protected the time I needed to pen this tome. Also, Greg Kaiser was the first of this austere Blanchard club to believe in me.

Mary Foley, author of *Bodacious!*, and Marta Brooks, co-author of *The Leadership Legacy*, poured over every page, suggesting, editing, encouraging, cajoling, and providing constructive feedback. Andrew Wampler, the architect of words and sentences, eliminated dangling participles and misplaced commas I so frequently scribed. Finally, Elaina Loveland has applied masterful insight into language and words, taking this manuscript from a collection of musings to a book that will touch your heart.

Thank you all. Your influence in my life has crafted for me a fascinating and rewarding journey.

This has truly been a "Gung Ho" experience.

Ray A. Snyder

August 2005

This book would never have been penned were it not for Megan. I have cherished the gift of calling her my daughter every moment of her life. She is my inspiration and the composer of my heart's song as it is played on these pages.

By Ken Blanchard
Co-author of *The One Minute Manager*

Wherever I go, people ask me about "balance."

Twenty years ago, I would take their questions to be about "balancing" the relationship between operations and marketing, "balancing" the books, or "balancing" their long and short game on the golf course. Never would I have thought they were asking about the "balance" between work and home life.

Times have changed a lot in recent decades. People at work are more focused than ever on their lives at home. Most compartmentalize their relationships to in be either one or the other, but rarely do people consider that the things they do at work can successfully be done at home, too!

I met Ray Snyder in the late 1980s. He was facilitating leadership seminars for our company, and even then had a vision of merging workplace leadership skills with those that people successfully use at home. We talked often about family, work, and the relationship between the two realms. The results of those talks, Ray's decades of experience with the corporate and government worlds, and delightful storytelling he mastered by teaching small children about faith and values for twenty years, are presented here in *The Business of Families*.

This isn't a book about just families. It's a reference about our lives at work and at home. Each chapter teaches a skill that, when mastered at work, can be applied at home with tremendous success and effectiveness. The idea that we have to separate our lives at work from our existence with our families is a fallacy. We all have a golden opportunity to merge the two.

Every person, be it a father, a mother, a child, a neighbor, a friend, or a co-worker, has the foundation to build relationships at home and at work into fruitful and lasting commitments to one other.

The Business of Families goes so much further than a simple documentary about leadership skills. There are practical activities, exercises, and resources to use with your family. Each chapter describes a component of leadership that may be developed at home. Many have an activity to facilitate that development, not to mention stories that will have you rolling in the floor when recognize *your* family and co-workers in the conversations.

Enjoy our journey, folks. What a delight it is to search for "balance" and find the prescription for it in the pages of *The Business of Families.*

CHAPTER ONE

Have you ever heard a conversation like this before?

Father: "There is no way I'll allow any son of mine to wear a sissy earring!"

Son: "But Dad, everybody's got one! What's the big deal? I think it looks great and my friends wear one all the time."

Father: "Well, if your friends jumped off the bridge, would you follow them?"

Son: "That's stupid, Dad. Of course I wouldn't."

Father: "Then why wear an earring like everyone else? Haven't I taught you to think for yourself and not follow the crowd? Besides, what is a potential employer going to think when you show up all decked out in pretty jewelry?"

Son: "Come on, Dad! I'm a senior in high school, for goodness sake. Even the manager at McDonalds has one. You're living in the dark ages."

Father: "The dark ages weren't so bad, so don't knock them. At least we didn't go around piercing body parts and wearing holey clothes."

Son: "Well, what about your ponytail in college, huh? And what about Granddad's Lucky Strikes rolled up in his T-shirt sleeve? And what about mom's flower tattoo that nobody but you ever sees? I've seen pictures of her wearing dresses shorter than anyone wears today!"

Father: "That's different, son, and you know it. Those were different times with different values. You kids are doing radical things that make no sense. And don't talk about your mother like that!"

Son: "Well, you shouldn't talk about me and my friends like that either! Just because we dress differently and act differently than you doesn't mean we are bad people. Why can't you see that?"

***

Why Can't You Believe What I Believe?

Values, the beliefs about life that drive our behaviors, have been around since the beginning of time. Organizational values are documented in the written word of Biblical text as early as Cain and Abel in Genesis. You can follow the impact of organizational values throughout history from the stately empires of ancient Egypt through the teachings of spiritual leaders who lived thousands of years ago up to today's Fortune 500 companies.

Our values are best understood when they are articulated. For example, even an old and established company like Caterpillar's Track Type Tractors Division has articulated values along with behaviors to demonstrate those values within the company. New and progressive companies such as AOL and Google also articulate values. The concept of values is not lost even on governmental organizations such as the Bureau of Alcohol, Tobacco, and Firearms and the U.S. Navy.

Unfortunately, values in many organizations are often simply "words on the wall" rather than serious guidelines that effect the way they conduct business.

Employee: "How can we do that? Our number one value is supposed to be that our employees are important to us! Now you want to layoff 10,000 of them in one fell swoop!"

Manager: "You tell me how we can keep our income statement in the black without losing people, and I'll be glad to listen."

Employee: "You and I have both known that staying in the black is important, but profitability in just one off-year is no reason to take such rash action."

Manager: "So you're saying it doesn't matter what our stockholders think, am I right?"

Employee: "Of course not, but I am saying that I thought shareholder value was somewhere behind taking care of our employees."

Manager: "Well, I guess you are just wrong. They don't call me 'chainsaw' for nothing. All this other nice stuff about employees, morale, and customer satisfaction is nothing more than pure, unmitigated psychobabble. Shareholder value reigns supreme when I'm in charge."

Employee: "So I've been told."

Conversations like this one have been held in numerous widely publicized corporate restructuring endeavors. What is actually happening is not usually a difference in values but most often is a difference in the ranking of those values and the behaviors that demonstrate them. Unfortunately, employees and customers are usually the first people to be re-ranked when organizations find themselves in financial turmoil.

Conflict arises when someone practices a value that the organization doesn't share or when someone sacrifices a higher order value to strengthen a lower order one. Let me explain.

The order of values determines which people might be compromised if the compromising behavior strengthens one higher up the list.

I have worked on identifying my personal core values. Over the course of a two-year journey, I came up with these:

1. **Ethical** — Doing the right thing
2. **Excellence** — Doing it very well
3. **Collaborative** — Working with others
4. **Financial** — Making and giving money
5. **Fun** — Enjoying myself

These five values are practiced in three arenas of my life. They are:

- **Personal** — My family life and friendships
- **Professional** — My business life
- **Spiritual** — My inner journey with God

The order of these values is no accident. This ranking gives me great leeway in determining when to strengthen and when to sacrifice a value. For example, if I were presented with the opportunity to send two invoices to a company for conducting one keynote speech, knowing full well that I could pull it off without ever getting caught, it would strengthen my number four value—*financial*. However, it would sacrifice my number one value—*ethical*. Since my rule about values dictates that a lower order value can never be strengthened at the expense of a higher order value, the decision is straightforward: send only one invoice.

If presented with an opportunity to work with a volunteer service organization to teach strategic planning and assist them in identifying growth opportunities in their community, I would decide that this will strengthen my spiritual journey while supporting my *ethical* and *excellence* values. However, it sacrifices my number four *financial* value. Since a higher order value is being strengthened at the expense of a lower order value, my decision to volunteer becomes acceptable.

Once these values are identified and behaviors are agreed upon within a family, life becomes much clearer for everyone. In my home, a demonstration of the top two values in our spiritual life is that we attend church services on Sunday. That behavior has been discussed and accepted by everyone in the family. Sunday morning arguments about whether to sleep in or go to church rarely occur because the behavior and the value are part of our lives and are near the top of our list.

Even simple behaviors, such as expressing gratitude for small flavors, cutting the "bones" off of a small child's breakfast toast, and picking up dirty clothes instead of trashing a bedroom can demonstrate values considered important by the family.

Just as it is in organizations that do not identify, support, or act consistently in practicing their values, families can suffer the same chaos this ambivalence creates.

One example of this might be the scenario below:

Mother: "I can't believe you did that! You said you were going to the mall with Julie. I just got a call from Julie's mom asking to speak to her. Where have you been?"

Daughter: "We just went with some friends to the beach, mom. Don't worry, we were fine."

Mother: "You are fifteen years old, and you know you don't have permission to go to the boardwalk at night. We've discussed this many times. You know about all the drugs and alcohol that are out there at night. What were you thinking?"

Daughter: "Come on, Mom. We weren't using drugs or drinking. We were just hanging out with our friends.

If I'd ask you for permission, you'd have said no. What was I supposed to do, tell the truth?"

Mother: "I thought that was important in our family."

In this conversation, which nearly all parents have experienced with their teenager at some point in life, what's really happening is the teen is questioning the family's values. Most teens won't fall prey to life threatening use of drugs or alcohol, but that's exactly where most parents will take this conversation, rather than a re-alignment of values.

Here is another hypothetical situation:

Wife: "You are impossible to live with! Just look at this place. We've both been working our butts off all week-long. We finally have the weekend to spend some time with each other, and you think it's a great time to spend the day with your buddies. Did you forget you had a wife at home? Do you think this household just runs itself? What's it going to take to get a little consideration from you?

Husband: "That is totally unfair. I've worked just as hard as you have this week and need the weekend to wind down. Nobody ever said we were joined at the hip, did they? Why can't I have a little fun after a long week? What makes running the household on the weekend the most important task on the planet?"

Later, the conversation might continue like this:

Wife: "Well, I thought your family was the most important group of people on the planet, but obviously I was mistaken. Did you have a nice time telling jokes, drinking beer, and scratching yourself? I wouldn't know. I've been cleaning the house and working on Jimmy's science project all day."

Husband: "Listen, I'm the man of this house, and you have no right to talk to me that way."

Wife: "Well, maybe you should start acting like a husband and a father to us, rather than just a man to your friends."

Husband: "How dare you question my commitment to my family! You are being totally unreasonable."

Wife: "Keep this up, James, and I'll show you unreasonable like you've never seen it before."

Unreasonable. Irresponsible. Uncaring. Selfish. Unfair. Wrong. These are words we use when our perceived, and supposedly agreed upon, value systems are being compromised. The couple in this conversation probably doesn't have a conflict around which values are important to them and their family. Their conflict is rooted in the ranking of those values. Both of them love their children and each other and both work hard to provide for their family. They also both recognize the need for strong parenting and home-making skills. They both understand the need for rest and relaxation and enjoy spending time with their friends.

The problem was that each of them ranked these values differently that Saturday.

To begin your journey identifying the values and behaviors you hold important in your family, start with your behaviors. Most husbands, wives, parents, and children would say that the relationships they share with one another are the most important things in their lives. When challenged with a calendar and a checkbook, however, the time and money they spend often reveals behaviors that demonstrate substantially different values. This difference doesn't make a person bad, but it does raise the question of inconsistency between spoken words and demonstrated behaviors, the very same issue that causes chaos and distrust in organizations.

Try writing twenty things that you and each member of your family do on a routine basis. Remember to filter these things through your five senses, making them behaviors. Each person should write behaviors that are not only *personally* demonstrated, but also behaviors each *other* member of the family exhibits.

Armed with literally hundreds of observable behaviors, you can begin the process of classifying them into values. My values are listed as one word, but you can use phrases or even full sentences to describe your values. After classifying all the behaviors into no more than ten different values, try to cull the list into a more manageable five or six "big picture" values. Then go back to your behaviors and list them under each value. This inventory shows how you live, not just talk about, your values with each other.

Next, rank these values from one to five or six, and classify the behaviors into categories of your lives. For example, my professional life is my work. While my teenagers' professional life is school, my wife's professional life includes both her job and community activities. My spiritual life revolves around my relationship with God and church, and my next-door neighbor's spiritual life includes a significant commitment he has to counseling the families of terminally-ill children.

Once your values are identified, ranked, and supported with behaviors, you can begin the process of deciding which behaviors should be enhanced and which should be reduced or eliminated. You'll probably even come up with a few new behaviors that should be added if you're going truly to live by your values within your family.

In Charleston, South Carolina, we have a very old and rickety two-lane bridge. It is more than three miles long and stands one hundred and fifty feet above the harbor. As a child, I can remember my little sister ducking down in the back seat of our two-tone 1967 Chevy Impala every time we traveled across this bridge going to the beach for a family outing. It was a terrifying experience for her (much to my sadistic and brotherly delight).

I've asked literally thousands of people who have traveled that bridge if they've ever hit the guardrails. Only two have responded affirmatively. I exclude those two from this example.

The remaining multitude of people who have never hit the guard rails are asked how they would feel if forced to go across the bridge if it were simply two lanes of concrete that had a flat edge dropping straight into the harbor. Of course, no one wants to travel on that hair-raising trip.

With a smile on my face I ask, *"Why?"*

You may be able to predict the response I got: "Because I might fall off. It would be a nightmare. How could I stay safe on a bridge with no guardrails?"

My question about values is exactly that. The guardrails in families are values, behaviors, and expectations. How can anyone stay safe not knowing exactly where the limits and boundaries of behaviors exist?

When the boundaries of family values, behaviors and expectations aren't clear or understood, it can cause emotional stress. Family members dealing with stress my have these kinds of thoughts:

- "I don't know where to begin. My marriage is in shambles. My children hate me. I'm about to lose my job. I haven't spoken to my family in a year. I've tried to do the right thing all my life. Who can teach kids anything these days? Their friends and MTV have more impact on them than I do. The only way I can get through the day is knowing I can find a little peace with a few drinks and an occasional weekend joint. How was I to know my son was doing the same thing?"

- "We dropped them off at Sunday school every week until they were ten. Why do they think church is a joke now? I was so busy working on my lawn and garden projects that I just didn't have time for PTA or ball games. Is that any reason for my kids to have no interest in school or team sports? I've got a busy life too, you know. You'd think my ex-wife would have understood that instead of finding someone else who could stroke her ego, wouldn't you?"

- "My youngest daughter just got caught shoplifting ten dollars worth of makeup at the mall. She believes just because I wrote a bad check on a canceled account last year at Christmastime that it gives her permission to take whatever she wants for free too. Can you believe the audacity and stupidity of that child? Even my parents are being jerks. I've been trying to manage a family for fifteen years. I've got a life of my own too, don't I? They are retired. Why can't they come visit us instead of us having to pack the clan in the car and spend half the weekend driving to visit them?"

- "People just don't have values like they used to, do they? Whatever happened to people understanding and appreciating their families?"

Whatever happened to people understanding and appreciating their values? That's a great question we should all ask of ourselves and our families.

Give it a try. Do the values thing. You might just amaze yourself and your family with how much you really have in common with each other when you make a commitment to living and being held accountable for demonstrating your shared values in your daily lives.

CHAPTER TWO

August 27, 1975
Charleston, South Carolina
"Now what are we going to do? We've been married all of one week, I'm unemployed, and your father is not impressed. Well, maybe he is a little bit relieved that we won't be spending the next 20 years hopping around globe with the Air Force, but just being close to home for the rest of our lives won't put food on the table or pay the rent."

August 30, 1975
"I got the job, Kathy. I start tomorrow morning at Gingiss Formalwear in Northwoods Mall. It's just part-time for now, but I think I can make manager of the store in less than a year."

December 12, 1976
"I got the job Kathy. I start in a few weeks with Milliken in Barnwell, South Carolina. It's just a small town, but it'll be great experience working for a big company now. I'll spend six months as a management trainee, and given a few years I'll probably be running the place."

April 22, 1981
"I got the job Kathy. I start in a week as the new Training Manager for the South Carolina State Ports Authority. They've never had a Training Department, and I get to write my own ticket. It'll be great moving back to Charleston."

September 8, 1982
"I got fired today, sweetheart. They laid off 68 people, but since I'm a manager and training is always the first thing to go,

they just gave me severance pay until the end of the month and a good recommendation. What are we going to do?"

September 25, 1982

"I got the job, Kathy. I'll have to spend about two months in training, but then I'll be a Registered Representative for The Equitable Life Assurance. I know I've never sold anything other than in the mall, but I think I'll be good at this."

August 19, 1983

"I hate this job, Kathy. Every time I pick up the phone to make a cold call, it feels like the handset weighs fifty pounds. I guess I'm not cut out to be an insurance agent. Maybe I can start my own company and just do training."

November 12, 1986

"I love being my own boss, Kathy. I think we can grow the training business even more if Ed will quit his job in New Jersey and move here. It'll be great having our friends as next-door neighbors again. We can make twice as much money with two of us working at it."

May 23, 1987

"You know how much we love working with computers, Kathy. We're spending a couple of hours every day just helping our friends and business acquaintances hook up their systems. Ed and I want to open a computer store. We've even got a great name—Network Computer Systems. I'll keep doing the training side of the business, and Ed will head up the computer side. It'll be like having a hobby and getting paid for it."

November 3, 1988

"Ed is my second best friend in the whole world next to you, Kathy. I don't know how we're going to survive. Business stinks, and we're in debt up to our ears. I think Ed has a lead on a job. It'll be lonely being by myself again."

March 17, 1989

"You won't believe it Kathy. This guy named Ken Blanchard, who wrote a great book, is going to have me conduct a training session in Washington D.C. for his company. This job might be our big break."

June 28, 1993

"Now I understand Kathy. I can't say I've wasted time or squandered effort, but I sure do wish I'd been more intentional in my career choices. It looks like our ship has come in, and although I'm at the airport most of the time, I plan to sail on this journey. You've had incredible patience for eighteen years. It's about time I started acting like I have a plan. I love you."

February 3, 1997

"Kathy, have you ever been listening to someone speak or reading a book and it feels like the GE commercial with the light bulb is playing inside your brain? That happened to me last week. I was having dinner with Ken, and he was describing his journey with Blanchard Training and Development and the crossroads facing them now. It was like listening to Dickens's *A Christmas Carol*. He had a distinct past, a productive present, and a very uncertain future. While he was talking, our life together flashed before my eyes. We've had a meandering but fulfilling past, a great present, and even though our future looks bright, it could all crash around us in a heartbeat.

"Ken talks about these curves that look like the life-cycle of a business. I think they apply to our lives at home too. It's time we got smart about doing what we do for a purpose, not just doing things because they feel right in our gut."

"I love you too, Ray."

✿✿✿

Managing the Curves

F. Scott Fitzgerald said, "The test of a first-rate intelligence is the ability to hold two conflicting ideas in mind at the same time, and still retain the ability to function."

The first thirty-nine years of my life were lived in all capital letters. My career—or more aptly stated, careers—were relatively successful but occurred in a haphazard fashion. Whatever it was that I decided to do next was built upon improving what I had done last. The most significant focus of all my career changes was income.

Ken Blanchard and Terry Waghorn identified a derivative of the Sigmoid Curve as it is applied to business. Plotted on an X and Y axis with time graphed horizontally and success graphed vertically, they show that business will usually start out with little success and grow over time by improving its practices and processes. This representation is called the "Present Curve."

Successful organizations recognize that their continued success depends not on simply improving performance on current activities, but also on the creation of new and unproven activities. This new curve is most successfully initiated while success is still on an upward trend. Success in new ventures might follow the same pattern as the initial present curve. With tenacity, creativity, luck (defined as when opportunity and preparation meet), and resources, these new ventures will often begin to rise as successful results are realized. This rise is called the "Future Curve."

This idea isn't rocket science. The Sigmoid Curve describes the rise and fall of governments, the success and failure of business, the reliability of an automobile, and the birth, life, and death of a person. It also describes the life cycle of many families.

We instinctively understand these things when we raise children. God must really have a smile His face as he watches parents struggle with life's decisions about their children. Babies are born naked with no instructions. Most parents do the best they can with what they have, and most kids turn out just fine.

When little Johnny is about one year old, we began working on walking. This is Johnny's present curve. Over time, he gets better and better at walking, but Mom and Dad recognize the need for a future curve too. So we place a spoon in little Johnny's hand and begin self-feeding lessons. After a while, potty training becomes the future curve while walking and eating have transformed into Present Curve activities. Later, preschool, first grade, high school graduation, college, and careers become Future Curve interests.

These are all intentional activities that Johnny and his parents plan, discuss, and implement with great forethought. Finally, little Johnny is no longer little and goes out on his own starting a new family and career. Why is it at this point that the intentional focus on Future Curve activities that was so prevalent during his formative years now shifts to intense focus on Present Curve things and only cursory attention to his Future Curve?

The answer to this question is revealed when you study family traditions.

When America was an agrarian society and many of us lived in rural areas in farming communities, the Present Curve for most children was not much different than today. Children were born, learned to walk, talk, and feed themselves. They went to school and learned their family's values. The college and career segment of the Future Curve, however, was often redirected to working in the family business, trade, or farm. When little Johnny was raised seventy-five years ago, he did pretty much the same thing that little Johnny will do today. He started his own family, went to work, raised children, and progressed through his career as an extension of his present curve with very little focus on a future curve as it applied outside of the home. Future Curve activities in families are most often a function of past "proven" Future Curves, rather than true "unproven" endeavors.

We've learned in business that to be successful we need to focus on both curves. IBM learned this with their personal computer market. Kodak learned this in their battle with Fuji; Microsoft learned this while developing Windows. America Online learned this as they experienced tenfold growth in two years. Personally, I learned this only after thirty-nine years of experiencing it in the blind.

The challenge of successful business is the ability to expend resources from profitable operations to fund unproven future activities. Recognizing the potential growth that might be realized by doing something new is the capstone of an effective organization. It should be no different in our families.

Teaching children new and unproven skills is an important part of life. Teaching them why these new future skills are necessary is often overlooked. Successful families understand the need for both efficient and the effective skills and routines for day-to-day living, as well as the richness that can be added to their relationships by undertaking new and unproven challenges.

These new challenges can take the form of anything from learning to snow ski to joining a bowling league. Reading a new book every week or surfing the Internet to complete homework might be new and interesting things to do. Even turning off the television during dinner or taking an hour a week to play Monopoly would qualify as a future curve activity for most families.

Many things that families identify as a Future Curve activity will become a present curve activity over time. Just like learning to walk was once a Future Curve endeavor, for most of us it's now a Present Curve duty.

It's important that everyone in the family understands why you're doing things differently than before. Shaking things up (new Future Curve stuff) just for the sheer enjoyment of doing so will often cause strife and discontent. Shaking things up so that you can explore your futures together with your eyes wide open as to why you're doing new stuff, however, can be invigorating.

Today, little Johnny is Big Johnny. He works more than he should and doesn't get to spend nearly as much time with his wife and children as he wishes he could. They all understand, however, that each of them plays an important role in their family's Present Curve and Future Curve. The Future Curve they've identified is that their three children, now in middle and high school, will attend college, the first to do so in the history of either side of their family.

To make this happen, Johnny works a full-time day job and has started a small home business for nights and weekends. The five of them have figured out that the only way they'll fund their Future Curve is to work together to make it successful. Johnny and his wife are teaching their children the importance of intentionally committing their time and effort to being the best they can be every day as well as creating their future together.

Johnny never had the opportunity to sit in a boardroom, conduct a strategic planning session, or attend a business seminar. But he has many things figured out. His past is well known with no regrets. His present, with three teenagers at home, is hectic and fast-paced. His future is intentional.

CHAPTER THREE

December 12, 2001

Megan: "Paul, I know we've only been going together for six months, but I need to warn you about Christmas at our house. When we start to put the ornaments on the tree, Mom and Dad will have to tell you the story about every single ornament, starting with when Dad met Mom and had a clothespin angel attached to a dozen roses and ending with the ornaments we made last year. Just smile, and ask a few questions once in a while."

Paul: "Sure, it'll be fun. My family does it a whole different way."

Dad: "It looks better this year than it's ever looked in here!"

Megan: "Dad, you say that every year."

Dad: "You'd be disappointed if I didn't, sweetheart."

Megan: "I know Dad; it's what our family does."

Five minutes later....

Mary Ann: "It's my turn to put the angel on top of the tree."

Megan: "No it isn't either. You did it last year. It's my turn this year!"

Mary Ann: "Dad! Tell Megan it's my turn this year."

Megan: "Dad! Tell Mary Ann it's my turn this year."

Dad: "Girls, do we have to do this every year?"

Grinning ear-to-ear, in unison the girls respond, "Of course, Dad, it's what our family does!"

December 15, 7:00 p.m.

On the phone, Kathy whispers, "I understand. She's in the hospital in critical condition. It'll take a few hours to drive. We'll be there as soon as we can."

"Honey, great-grandmother is in the hospital, and they don't know if she's going to make it."

"Okay, let's make a few calls and hit the road."

"I'm glad I didn't have to ask if you thought we should go."

"This is family, sweetheart. It's what our family does."

December 18, 4:30 p.m.

"Grandma died."

"I'll get the car gassed up, and we can be on the way in a half-hour."

"It's what our family does."

December 19, 8:30 a.m.

"We'll be bringing a roast beef dinner over tonight if that's okay with you," offered my Mom this morning. "I know you'll be busy taking care of your family, and it's the least we can do to help out. It's what our family does."

December 25, 1997, 6:00 a.m.

At the foot of the bed with sleepy eyes and anticipating hearts, we read together, "And it came to pass in those days...."

1:30 p.m.

"Roll me over and tuck me in. That was the best meal I've had all year."

"You always eat too much of my dressing, and you always complain to me about cooking too much for the holidays!"

"You know, Mom, it's what our family does."

4:00 p.m.

"You better not pout, you better not shout, you better not cry, I'm telling you why..." we sing on the two-hour journey to the other Grandma's house. It's what our family does.

7:00 p.m.

"Do we have to open all these presents one at a time? It'll take forever. Can't *we please* open two at a time?" ask ten starry eyed, excited nieces and nephews in harmonious unison.

"One at a time, kids, and hugs and kisses after each one. It's what our family does."

"Robert, stop throwing the wrapping paper at Jim."

"Cliff, hug your Aunt Kathy."

"What do you say to Uncle Ray, Charles?"

"Did anyone get socks this year?"

"Where are the batteries?"

"I love this sweater."

"*No*, I won't model the pajamas in front of everyone!"

"This was the best Christmas ever!"

"That's what you say every year, Dad."

It's what our family does.

✿✿✿

Traditions

I recently facilitated a session on leadership with a dozen America Online employees in San Francisco. As I walked into their office area, I noticed fresh fruit, gourmet coffee, people smiling and discussing issues and plans as they walked through the hallways, and even a few pool players in the corner canteen overlooking Silicon Valley.

Three weeks earlier, I was working with a company and

its managers in a conference room that was a throwback from the 1950s, complete with instant coffee in plastic cups and broken audiovisual equipment. The week before that I read glowing evaluations of a three-hour customer service workshop from which people aired only complaints about the lack of refreshments for participants.

On another occasion while observing workers walking to work from the parking lot of a plant at a huge manufacturing facility in the Midwest, I felt as if a funeral was in progress. At 5:00 that afternoon, however, thousands of "freed subordinates" would have made Richard Petty proud.

AT&T has a day when all of the employees wear a yellow tie. At Milliken's Barnwell Mills, you feel naked without ear plugs hanging around your neck, even if you're not in the Weave Room. Folks at BMW wear polo shirts. At Ubique in Tel Aviv, lunch is catered for all employees in their Kosher kitchen so that everyone can discuss their business and personal life comfortably. Caterpillar managers read the newest and greatest leadership literature as it is published. ATF agents come to classes armed. GlaxoSmithKline managers do not.

It is fascinating to watch people enact organizational traditions in their daily routines. Whether it is eating fresh fruit at work, arriving early to get the most comfortable conference room seat, scarfing donuts and cappuccino on a break, or transforming a sorrowful sunrise shuffle into a ferocious foot race to freedom, people learn to count on and find stability in traditions.

These traditions often evolve into an expression of an organization's culture. It takes years to create or change culture. Like it or not, all organizations have one. It's like belly buttons; to be a human being, a belly button is your ticket onto the planet. To be an organization, regardless of its legal status as a corporation, government agency, school, church, or other entity, the ticket to its long-term existence is the creation of a culture.

Organizational culture molds the attitudes and beliefs that drive the behaviors of the people within it. Behaviors are observable actions. They represent the *true* nature of the organization, regardless of its "officially sanctioned" culture. For example, a company that promotes its open-door and two-way communication culture is sending a mixed message to its employees when secret meetings, rigid chain-of-command hierarchy, and blind copy e-mails are used.

On the other hand, an agency that is publicly committed to staying focused on its customers and the welfare of its employees will be seen as truthful when it adopts near-instant customer service response systems and wellness programs for its people.

The bottom line is that attitudes and beliefs communicate how organizations might *wish* to define their cultures. Behavior demonstrates the *reality* of that wish.

Families Are No Different

As children, we learn traditions that demonstrate the culture of our family. The conversations at the beginning of this chapter describe traditions practiced in times of grief and consolation, preparation for a holiday, and sharing of joy and celebration. Tradition is not limited, however, to the big things in life.

Saying grace, kissing before leaving, clearing the table, picking up your socks, and putting ketchup on rice and gravy are all traditions. Every family has their own set of traditions, and they are as diverse as the noses on our faces.

In times of stress and discontent, families find strength and security in practicing well-known traditions. Mary Ann, after a particularly grueling day at school, finds peace playing the piano while Mom or Dad sit quietly nearby and simply listen. Starting a meal without offering a prayer is a guaranteed prescription for indigestion. Reading the paper without a cup of coffee should be illegal. Going to bed without a goodnight kiss evokes insomnia.

Living one's daily life without being firmly grounded in routine tradition is chaotic.

I never realized what these small daily acts of life mean to my family until we had small children. It seemed that whenever we got a late start in the morning, everyone was all out-of-sorts for the balance of the day. Going more than a week without attending a worship service at church left us feeling edgy and quick-tempered. Going to bed angry with each other ensured exhaustion the following afternoon.

Watch what happens to people who travel infrequently as they take a solitary business trip. On about the third day of their travels, you'll notice a difference in their appearance, demeanor, and effectiveness at their job on the road. Their discontent often comes from an interruption of their daily traditions.

The best road-warriors create new traditions while traveling that they substitute for the family traditions they forego. Being a road-warrior myself, I've learned from the best of them.

Reading a hometown newspaper on-line while three thousand miles from home is a joy. Wake-up calls to home at the breakfast hour, regardless of your time zone, will bring a smile to everyone's day. Pictures of your family on the hotel night stand, breakfast at Burger King (okay, that's a stretch), and faxed copies of report cards are all tactics we invoke to stay connected to our families while away from them.

We should learn to *intentionally* do things like this at home. I teach my children to practice their traditions every day, regardless of where they are. Teaching children to intentionally maintain the traditions of your family, even when they are not *with* your family, is important. Encouraging children to call home when running late creates adult children who routinely check in with their parents. Consistently attending religious services of some sort, in spite of adolescent kicking and screaming, produces adults who find solace in worship. Megan has told me that she and Paul hold hands and pray *in restaurants*, something she had never done with anyone but our family. She said "It was weird, Dad, but it felt right."

When she said this I thought, *Yeah, Megan! Traditions Prevail!*

I was discussing this concept with a total stranger while sitting in the U.S. Airways club in San Francisco. As I was outlining this chapter on traditions, I found myself staying focused on the importance of consistent behaviors in families. He believes, rightfully so, that we learn our most important adult behaviors when we are children. This behavior includes parenting skills. This behavior includes values. This behavior includes attitudes about life. This behavior includes traditions. Passing these things on to our children when they are young teaches them to become good parents.

As an adult, I've practiced many family traditions without ever considering the reason why. Most of us unquestioningly adopt the traditions of our childhood families and continue them with our adult families.

"Why do you cut the roast in half before you cook it, Sweetheart?"

"Because that's the way my Mom did it. I never asked why."

"Let's ask your Mom the next time we visit."

"Heavens, honey. I guess your grandmother taught me to do it that way," her amused mother shared with her daughter a week later.

On the phone to Grandma, "Well, Sweetie, your great-grandmother did it that way, so I figured if it was good enough for her, it was good enough for me. Why don't you ask when you visit her next week?"

"Great-grandma, why did you always cut your roast in half before you cooked it?" queried the perplexed great-grandaugher."

"Well, Sugar, we were so poor that I didn't have a pot large enough to cook a roast without halving it. Why do you ask?"

This type of story has been around forever and is a perfect example of a tradition that was perpetuated across generations without question. Unfortunately, many family traditions include negative or destructive behaviors. A workman recently came to my front door to do an annual termite check of our home. We spoke a few minutes about the upcoming holiday, and it was as if a cloud entered the room.

No, it wasn't because some tragedy had befallen his family. He explained that he invented every reason in the world to excuse himself from family holiday celebrations because all they did was argue and fight. He said that since he was a small child, he could remember his great-grandparents, grandparents, and parents fussing and fighting about anything and everything during their holiday meals. Holidays, to him, were a painful tradition. How sad.

If you are fortunate enough to have loving parents or grandparents who are still alive, sit down with them one day soon and ask them to list for you the fifteen or twenty most memorable traditions they observed in *their* family as children. (Be sure to ask them about their childhood experiences, not your childhood experiences. You *know* the ones you remember. You're looking for what *they* remember.) If you don't have aged family members still alive, visit a nursing home and ask someone there. You'd be amazed at how you'll brighten someone's day by asking about *their* past.

You'll find it fascinating, especially as you talk to elders about their childhood. You may have to endure a few "walked five miles through the snow uphill both ways to get to school" stories, but you should find delightful traditions they experienced that may have been handed all the way down to your family today. You might even uncover a future tradition you'd like to start in your family.

Traditions don't happen quickly. They develop only when demonstrated consistently over time. Sporadic observance of a desired tradition produces only inconsistency and confusion. In your family, take the time to commit to paper the things that you want to become lifelong traditions. Write them down, think them through, cross-stitch them to hang on the wall, magnetize them to the refrigerator, and talk about them with each other. Most importantly, do them with the surety of gravity.

Gravity always works. We learned as small children not to defy it. Whether it is riding a bicycle or jumping a fence, we learned that we could count on both the positive and sometimes painful characteristics of gravity. We believe this principle without question, because gravity is one of the most consistent forces in our lives. So too, are traditions.

By proactively identifying and consistently observing positive traditions in your family, you can create the same security and consistency we've come to expect of gravity. Being grounded in tradition, which is demonstrated by behavior adds serenity, anticipation, and a daily "home base" to our lives. They are wonderful gifts to present to one another.

Intentional leadership does not happen by accident, nor does the positive influence traditions have on families. Be intentional with the ones you love, and your legacy to the world through your family will add richness and diversity to our society for generations to come.

CHAPTER FOUR

December 3, 1997
Rochester, New York
The Family Living Room
5:45 p.m.

"What a day! I walked in this morning and got hit squarely between the eyes with an emergency staff meeting and two reports that were due before noon. You should've seen it. It was a zoo in there. A dozen managers were loaded for bear just waiting for me to slip up. I only had twenty minutes to get ready, but they were blown away by the end of my presentation."

"That's nice, sweetheart."

"It was incredible. All the charts and graphs were perfect. It was like I was on stage in a Broadway play. People were listening, nodding their heads, and even taking notes. Even my boss, Marta, was smiling."

"Sounds like you had a great morning."

"That's an understatement. When the meeting was over, I hung around and spent a half-hour with Marta and three of the VPs. I tell you, honey, I was in my element. On my toes, animated, and speaking on the fly."

"That must have been exciting."

"That's only the beginning. I spent the rest of the morning with my people going over all the details of the staff meeting. We even compiled all the report data that was due at noon while we were meeting. It was great to see everyone pull together and talk around the table about all our options."

"So you had a banner day, didn't you?"

"It was incredible. This afternoon, Marta called another meeting and asked me to review the reports we had just completed ten minutes earlier for the marketing people. The Marketing VP took me aside after the meeting and asked me if I'd consider a transfer into his department. What a rush!"

"That's great, honey."

"I feel like I could dance all night. Let's call Greg and Lynn to celebrate. We can hit The Outback and devour one of those bloomin' onions."

"I don't think so, sweetheart. I've had a day just about like yours, and I'm exhausted."

"What happened? Did Jerry call you in to do another impromptu proposal for a client? That guy just never lets up, does he? Well, how'd it go? Did you knock their socks off? Maybe I can give you a few pointers on how to work a crowd. Can we call Greg and Lynn now?"

"Aren't you listening? I'm totally drained. I spent all morning shooting from the hip in a presentation to Jerry and a new client, and it took every last drop of my energy just to make it to 5:00 p.m. All I feel like doing right now is chilling out with the newspaper and a cup of cappuccino."

"Come on, honey. You'll feel a lot better after we get to Outback. It's always full of great people, and it's exciting just to be there."

Silence.

"What do you say, sweetheart? Are you game?"

"No."

"Why not? It'll be fun."

"Just give me some space, okay? It's been a bad day for me, and I don't need grief from you about going out again. Can't we just stay home and have a quiet evening?"

"If you say so. But you don't know what you're missing out on. Let's talk about it again in a few minutes. You'll feel better then."

Sigh.

Ten minutes later. . .

"Well, are you feeling better? Ready to call Greg and Lynn?"

Silence.

✿✿✿

Inside or Outside

The differences between extroverts and introverts are plentiful. Approximately 75 percent of Americans are extroverts. It comes as no surprise that the dichotomies in perspective, energy, and forethought are magnified when one must collaborate with the other.

The Myers-Briggs Type Indicator does an excellent job at measuring one's preferences between extroversion and introversion. The essential difference between the two is *not* how much one or the other talks, but instead how much forethought goes into speech before it happens. The extroverted husband and introverted wife in the conversation at the beginning of this chapter have completely different perspectives on their day.

The husband is energized, focused, and ready to take on the world after having spent a full day thinking on his feet and reacting to external stimuli. The introverted wife has experienced a similar day, but has a completely different reaction. She finds herself drained of all energy, overwhelmed, and ready to sit back and reflect on her thoughts.

An extrovert's essential stimulation is from the outer world of people, things, conversation, activities, and the environment.

An introvert's essential stimulation is from their inner world of thoughts, reflections, perceptions, ideas, and analysis. It's no wonder that when either is forced to spend significant time living in their non-preferred world, it is exhausting.

At work, introverts are great analysts and people watchers. Rarely does an introvert inject significant content into a conversation without first having spent a few moments reflecting on the words she might speak. Introverts often get 80 percent of a thought formed in their minds before speaking the remaining 20 percent. They might even create various permutations of how a conversation might develop before they even experience it.

Extroverts, on the other hand, usually get about 20 percent of a thought formed in their mind, and talk their way through the remaining 80 percent. It's a hoot watching extroverts argue with themselves in a conversation, because they can change their mind on a dime as new words are processed on the fly.

Both extroversion and introversion have valuable places in the workplace. Positions requiring significant analysis and evaluation of alternatives will most often be held by introverts. A job that requires quick responses, extensive verbal communication, and constant change will appeal mostly to extroverts. Many employees intuitively understand the differences between these two personality preferences and make small allowances for those who do not share their own preferred traits.

I've met some of the most energized and some of the most depressed people holding positions that either match or mismatch their preference toward extroversion or introversion. Bill is a senior department manager in a high-tech organization. He is an off-the-scale extrovert, and like me, rarely has a thought he hasn't talked about. He is in charge of all training, development, employee orientation, and public relations. Bill is in his element when speaking to the Rotary Club, welcoming new employees, teaching leadership skills to managers, and conducting press briefings. By the end of a full day of these activities, he feels like he could run a marathon.

George, another senior department manager in that same organization, is a died-in-the-wool introvert. He never met an idea he couldn't think about. Unfortunately, his job requires instant response to production and scheduling crises morning, noon, and night. His e-mail box is routinely full. He facilitates no less than four meetings every day and has two staff assistants who try to protect his time with little success. George is so over-whelmed that he is routinely near exhaustion.

In families, the same phenomenon exists. It must be a law of nature that introverts marry extroverts. Another rule seems to be that their children will also be all over the board on extroversion and introversion. Watch what happens in families where an introverted spouse works outside the home and an extroverted spouse works at home.

The introvert, having spent an entire day in an extroverted business world, arrives home to the extroverted partner who has lived in an introverted world all day. AS the introvert walks in the door, one-sided conversation proceeds at a breakneck pace. Activities of the day, problems experienced at home, children's behaviors, and every tidbit of bottled up minutia spills from the extroverted lips of the stay-at-home spouse.

The extroverted spouse, however, observes the introverted business-career spouse walk in the door with her tail dragging fifteen feet behind her. This partner plops in the chair, sips something cool to drink, and fumbles with the clicker to find the evening news. Of course, the problems of the day fill the air while the verbal thoughts of the moment quickly become overwhelming to the "plopped" spouse. Finally, one of the two responds:

"Aren't you listening to me? I've been here all day waiting for you to come home and talk with me about this. Can't you do something other than sit there like a bump on a log?"

Or

"Can you just put a sock in it for a few minutes? I've been fighting fires since I got up this morning, and I just need a few minutes to wind down before you hit me with every problem that's reared its ugly head today! Just chill out for a few minutes, okay!?"

No wonder most arguments in families begin within thirty minutes of members' arrival home from school or work. It's important for extroverts to realize that introverts need downtime to re-group and re-energize. It's also important for introverts to recognize extroverts' need to discuss and analyze verbally their activities of the day. In my family, we've come up with a fairly decent system to manage these differences.

Kathy, a turbo introvert, is given the space she needs to think and re-group, especially after spending significant time responding to an extroverted world. I, the verbal extrovert, plan my quiet time (even extroverts need space sometimes) around her down time two or three times a day.

Kathy, on the other hand, plans to live in my extroverted world during meals, car rides, and upon my arrival home from a trip. I also sling my "extroverted slime" toward other extroverts whenever I feel the need to talk about ideas or discuss issues when Kathy is unavailable.

We primarily make these allowances for each other to avoid the pain and suffering we jointly inflict by imposing our extroverted or introverted nature on the other at inappropriate times. We've learned to adapt this little trick to our children as well.

Mary Ann, a delightful introvert, needs thirty minutes with a book, TV, or computer game when she arrives home from school. She is at her best when given an opportunity to recharge her batteries by "thinking about things" before having to do homework, practice the piano, or talk extensively about her day.

Megan, on the other hand, needs intensive interaction immediately upon arrival home from school. She is so energized after having spent the day with her friends and talking about everything under the sun that interests a teenager, that if we forced her to "chill out" for a half-hour before being allowed to interact with her world at home, she would be bouncing off the walls.

Understanding these differences has also presented interesting opportunities to manage marital conflict. In an argument with my wife, a tape recorder might reveal that 90 percent of the air time is filled with my voice. I've learned that her *silence does not equal anger* when arguing a point. Kathy also understands the need to say something once in awhile, even if she hasn't thought it all out, just to keep me engaged in the conversation. Her best thoughts and reflections don't make it into the conversation until after she has assessed and planned potential responses. This tact has also revealed a fascinating phenomenon in our relationship.

I call it the "I told you that" syndrome.

Have you ever been told that you were previously informed of something that is getting ready to happen or already passed, while you apparently forgot all about it? Not simple things, like "take out the trash," but the serious stuff, like "the boss is coming for dinner Wednesday night." We found ourselves in the midst of many "I Told You That" situations in the early years of our marriage. My response would often be, "Kathy, I've never heard those words together in one sentence in my whole life!" Her rejoinder or would be, "Well, I thought about telling you!"

We can laugh about these "introverted brain burps" today, but at the time, they were fairly serious conflicts. Recognizing and allowing for the differences we share in families can add tremendous joy to our existence together. Extroverts need airtime to vent their ideas to the room. They get their energy by explaining their thoughts and surrounding themselves with people and activity. Introverts need space to think about their ideas. They get their energy from peace and solitude.

Enabling your family members to operate at their peak means granting the audience and activity, or space and serenity needed. It's also important to understand that extroverts have the capacity to behave like an introvert and introverts can take on extroverted characteristics. Remember, personality is defined by preferences, not by ironclad rules.

Educate one another about these preferences by watching a few movies. Henry Fonda's 1956 academy award-winning film *Twelve Angry Men* spotlights extroverted characters in the Garage Man, Messenger, Ball Fan, and Ad Man. The introverted Foreman, Stockbroker, Slum Kid, and Old Man provide wonderful balance.

Extroversion and introversion are demonstrated in cartoons. Dennis the Menace, Catbert, Hagar, and Marmaduke all think out loud. General Halfrack, Dilbert, Linus, and Cathy are all thinkers before they speak. What a delightful experience you will have watching films and cartoons with your loved ones while learning how to cope with the differences in your personalities.

As it is with all the Myers-Briggs Type Indicator (MBTI) measured preferences, diversity in personalities adds richness to relationships. It's a real challenge for us to accept and embrace people who think and behave differently than us. For your family to be truly loving and compassionate with each other, however, it is a prerequisite that you acknowledge and allow those differences not because of the divisiveness they cause, but because of the greatness they encourage.

As a footnote to this chapter, take note that this entire book, written by an extrovert personified, is being dictated directly to a computer using Dragon System's NaturallySpeaking software. My fingers just can't seem to keep up with my mouth, but my computer performs that task with flair!

CHAPTER FIVE

January 16, 1988
A conversation between Ray and Kathy

Kathy: "You and Ed are doing lots of neat stuff on the computer. Would you teach me how to use that, what do you call it, word...processing?"

Ray: "Sure sweetheart, I'm an instructor par excellence. I'll be glad to teach you how to use word processing. Let's start off with the big picture."

Kathy: "Maybe you should just tell me how to make it work."

Ray: "No, I think you need to understand and how everything fits together first."

Kathy: "Okay, if you think so. But I really wish you just teach me what to do first."

Ray: "Trust me on this one. You'll never master everything you need to know about word processing and using this system if you don't get the big picture up front."

Kathy: "If you insist."

Ray: "Great. What we have is an IBM PC compatible running at 16 MHz. It has a 40 MB hard drive and 4 MB of random access memory. You talk to the computer by typing on the keyboard and it talks back to you by reflecting what you type on the screen. The first thing you're going to do is figuratively to open a file drawer as if the computer were a four drawer file cabinet. That's called a change directory command. Then you're going to type in the name of a command, executable, or batch file to start word processing. That's kind of like pulling out the word processing file from the appropriate file drawer. When you start the program you won't be working in DOS anymore, you'll be working in WordPerfect 5.0."

Kathy: (Interrupting) "Whoa! What buttons...do I punch... to word process?"

Ray: "Type CD\WP50 and press Enter. Then type WP and press Enter. That will start the word processing program."

Kathy: "Thank you, you may leave now."

So I left. I was fairly ticked off that she didn't appreciate my efforts to teach her how use the computer. (I didn't show her where the F3 key was, however, so she wouldn't be able to get help on her own from the computer). Ten minutes later, she called me back.

Kathy: "How do I print what I've typed here?"

I saw that she'd typed a paragraph and figured out things like word wrap, backspace, and the arrow keys.

Ray: "Sure sweetheart, printing is important if you want people to be able to read what you've written (pre-e-mail days in 1988). Let's start off with the big picture."

Kathy: "Maybe you should just tell me what to do next."

Ray: "Trust me on this, sweetheart. I've used computers for years, and you've got to understand how it all fits together before you can ever learn the details."

Kathy: "If you insist."

Being the dummy that I am, and a slow learner to boot, I charged ahead.

Ray: "This is a Panasonic KXP 4450 laser printer. It has I MB of random access memory, and works just like a copier. Instead of placing the original on a plate of glass, you send the original to the printer through a centronics parallel port on the back of the computer. It makes a copy of what you typed and prints it out on regular paper. You've got to make sure the on—line light is lit at all times and that the paper tray is firmly seated on the side of the printer."

Kathy: (Interrupting) "*Whoa!* What buttons...do I punch... to print?"

Ray: "Type Shift F7 and then the number one. That will print your document."

Kathy: "Thank you, you may leave again."

That was ten years ago. She has not called me back since. How ungrateful can a person be when I was just trying to help?

✿✿✿

How We Learn...or...Just the Facts, Ma'am.... Just the Facts...

or...Where Are We Going With This?

Carl Jung, Katherine Briggs, and Isabel Myers pioneered research in personality differences. Between the three of them, they identified eight different preferences from which everyone chooses four. These preferences, explained in the Myers-Briggs Type Indicator (MBTI), have been studied and applied to business for decades. Two of the dichotomies measured on the MBTI are Sensor vs. Intuitive.

Sensors are people who prefer to learn in sequential order. They gather details and arrange them in a way that builds to a complete understanding of the whole picture. People who prefer sensing as a way of learning often gravitate toward positions in organizations that recognize and reward this trait. You will find them excelling at engineering, banking, accounting, programming, and a myriad of other jobs that thrive in the mastery of details.

People who prefer Intuition as a way of learning often choose careers in writing, graduate teaching, artistry, music, politics, and the legal profession. These people learn best by first understanding the global perspective of whatever it is they do, then backing themselves into the details they must master to excel.

Observing a briefing or committee report in organizations is a delightful experience when filtered through these two preferences. Sensors will often present their information in a logical and sequential fashion. Their presentation begins with a historical perspective and builds one step at a time to a logical conclusion. The last few slides of their briefing links all the details together into a nice, neat package that can only be understood if the listener has been paying attention to the details first presented.

An Intuitive presentation takes an entirely different tract. Intuitives will often start with the conclusion. These presentations begin with an overview of the entire briefing. Serious Intuitives will even forget or ignore the details of the historical perspective, delving right into how their efforts are linked to or impact other areas of the organization. In other words, an Intuitive starts with the big picture and fills in the salient details.

Understanding the differences in these two preferred learning styles can greatly enhance relationships in families. Elementary school teachers often study these styles, and many apply learning theory in classrooms. The best teachers will start their lessons with an overview, begin again with the details, summarize occasionally by linking the details to the original overview, then plow back into the details.

Parents, friends, children, and spouses should do no less. Take a strong look at the missed communications you've experienced in your family in the past few months. Sensors often find themselves tuning out when Intuitives begin their conversation with the big picture, knowing full well that they can check back in when the details start to appear later on. Intuitives might get frustrated while listening to a Sensor explain details one step that time. They will often listen half-heartedly to the prerequisite details thinking that they will understand how it all fits together in a little while.

The opportunities to misunderstand one another are plentiful when two people share different preferences in learning. Effective members of families take great strides in understanding the learning styles of those they love. The child who can't grasp basic addition can be seen at the dining room table with a parent pushing two apples next two more apples to make four. An Intuitive child can then instinctively understand two plus two when she sees the "big picture" of four apples all together.

Another interesting dynamic of a Sensing learning style is the need to experience what's being learned with one or more of the five senses. Creative or conceptual ideas are often alien to sensing persons until they can see, hear, feel, touch, or smell the concept. This phenomenon comes alive when you watch a Sensor put a bicycle together fresh out of the box. Although Intuitives will often skip to the page with the blown up schematic and start to work, Sensors will read every instruction and go to step number one, following every detail in sequential order until the bike is finished.

It's interesting to note that both Sensors and Intuitives will assemble the bicycle. Intuitives simply have a few parts left over, which they are convinced have been shipped in the box just to frustrate them.

The differences between Sensors and Intuitives are evident wherever we look. It's the foundation for most situation comedies. We've all laughed ourselves silly at Jack Tripper trying to get Sissy to understand something. Jack says, "There is more than one way to skin a cat," to Sissy's response, "Why do you want to hurt the cat?"

Who can forget Sergeant Joe Friday's famous Sensor line: "Just the facts, ma'am, just the facts"?

Try asking a Sensor for directions. What you'll get is a detailed list of exactly what to do in easy to follow steps as you traverse from a starting point to an ending point. It's often drawn or written on paper or demonstrated by pointing to an imaginary spot on the wall or even tracing your route on the palm of a hand. Intuitive directions, on the other hand, take the form of reference to landmarks, "you've gone too far if…" statements, and vague assumptions about the distance or time it takes to arrive.

The comedy in family conversation can quickly turn to frustration and stress if the differences in communication and learning styles aren't understood and appreciated. Especially frustrating is a parent with a different learning style than his child.

Otto Kroeger and Janet Thuesen, authors of *Type Talk* and *Type Talk at Work*, do a wonderful job of explaining all the preferences and personality types in a variety of venues as they are identified by the Myers-Briggs Type Indicator.

It is possible to force people to learn in ways that do not address their preferred learning style. It's also frustrating for both the teacher and the student. A healthy alternative to judging others because of their difference in preferred learning style is to acquire skills that allow you to communicate effectively in a way that you can both understand and be understood. For Sensors, this goal might mean developing summarization skills that partially explain the conclusion at the beginning of a conversation. For Intuitives, this task may be a study in list making, detailing, and outlining.

Even reading outside of your normal comfort zone can enhance your communication skills. Sensors are notorious consumers of magazines. Intuitives devour novels. Sensors gravitate toward history and how-to books. Intuitives search the shelves for creative, unusual or innovative topics.

As young children, we observe both teaching styles in our literature. A child's storybook will most often be written from a Sensor's perspective with wonderful Intuitive illustrations that link the details to the big picture. Unfortunately, as grown-ups, our books have very few pictures.

Be aware of the differences in Sensors' and Intuitives' approaches to change. Sensors embrace things that can be replicated over time. Improving a process or activity to its most efficient form is a Sensor's challenge. To a Sensor, perfection is something that works efficiently and effectively again and again.

Intuitives often shake things up just for the sheer enjoyment of doing things differently. It's not unusual for a Sensor to arrive home from work and find the furniture completely rearranged just because the Intuitive partner thought it would be interesting, and was bored with the old arrangement. Recognizing and appreciating the need for variety by Intuitives and the need for stability by Sensors is a challenge for the whole family.

The most fulfilling relationships will display both Sensing and Intuitive learning and communication styles. Richness and fulfillment come from the absolute delight you can share as you learn to appreciate the diversity of personalities in your family. Judging each other because of your differences is destructive. Cherishing each other's unique perspective will add depth and wonderment to the privilege you share in living together.

CHAPTER SIX

November 27, 2002
Denver, Colorado
A conversation between Michael and Susan

Michael: "Well, it looks like the night will be shot for Aaron. We've already got three inches of snow on the ground and more forecast late tonight."

Susan: "I know it looks kind of bleak right now, Michael, but this is a big night for Aaron. Julie's Mom spent all last weekend making a new dress for her."

Michael: "I know, Susan, it stinks. But our job as parents isn't to give in to our children when their safety is at risk."

Susan: "I know that. But we have snow here all winter long. It's not that bad, and I think our job as parents includes teaching Aaron how to manage responsible risk and take care of himself when we're not around."

Michael: "That'll be kind of hard to do when he and Julie are laid up in hospital rooms. I can see it's not that bad out there now, but it could turn nasty before midnight."

Susan: "But the dance is only two miles away. How would you feel if your big date was indiscriminately jerked away from you without any regard for your personal feelings? He'll be absolutely embarrassed if he has to cancel his night out and it'll be even worse if we have to drive him. Come on Michael, he's a senior in high school."

Michael: "I don't care if he's a senior in college. I don't think he should be driving tonight. Although our decisions aren't always liked by everyone, being in a popularity contest is not a parent's job. We've got to stand together on this and be role models for Aaron. He might be mad or embarrassed now, but he'll appreciate our decision when he gets older."

Susan: "How can you be so insensitive? We're not having a blizzard out there, only a few inches of snow. The roads will be clear and we can tell him about driving slowly and safely. I know you've already spent time with him teaching him how to drive on slippery roads. He'll be just fine. I can remember my parents making decisions that embarrassed or hurt me, and I never did understand them, even when I got older."

Michael: "Sure, Susan, but you understand things with your heart, not your head. Aaron's different. I'm not willing to sacrifice his potential safety just so he can have a good time on a date."

Susan: "This isn't just any date, Michael. Other than the prom, this is the biggest social event of his senior year."

Michael: "Can't you see my point of view? I think it's a risk to let him drive tonight. It's only logical that one of us should drive him and Julie to the dance."

Susan: "You're not seeing my point of view! I think they'll be perfectly safe, and this'll be a great opportunity to demonstrate our trust to them both. Think

	about how these kids have anticipated tonight. It's
	important to them, and we should support them."
Michael:	"Can't you think with your head, Susan!"
Susan:	"Can't you feel with your heart, Michael!"

✿✿✿

Heads or Hearts

In this chapter on the Myers-Briggs Type Indicator (MBTI), we look at calamitous situations that seem impossible because of a difference in perspective on decision making. The two scales of decision-making measured on the MBTI are Thinking vs. Feeling.

Thinkers are wonderful analysts. Feelers demonstrate great compassion. Thinkers place great value on truth and logic. Feelers embrace peace and harmony. Thinkers weigh the pros and cons of a situation so that they might choose the *correct* course of action. Feelers seek to understand the people and emotions of a situation so that they might choose the *right* thing to do.

This is the only scale on the Myers Briggs Type Indicator that has a distinct sexual bias. Two-thirds of men are thinkers. Two-thirds of women are feelers. It's no wonder that in business, feeling men and thinking women find themselves swimming upstream against the tide.

In American society, most businessmen are expected to be logical and analytical, to the point of sometimes appearing cold and heartless. It is anticipated that many businesswomen will most likely make decisions and manage their job with compassion and emotion, seeking harmony and reducing conflict when possible. Not only are these expectations unrealistic, but they can be downright destructive in organizations.

Mary Brooks, the operations director for a Fortune 500

company in Virginia, holds an engineering degree and is one of the most dynamic people I've ever met. She runs her department with sage wisdom and is respected as a professional in her field. She is a wonderful analyst, and has a knack for interpreting short-term data in a way that accurately forecasts long-term performance. Her people think she's great. Unfortunately, her boss thinks she's too much of a taskmaster.

Mark Eastman, the vice president of operations, was hired because of his successful leadership during an ugly downsizing at another Fortune 500 company. Under Mark's leadership, the company turned what could have been a public relations nightmare into a stakeholders dream by ensuring that every affected employee received training, assistance, relocation services, and three months of career counseling. Many terminated employees actually felt as if it was a positive experience in their lives. From day one, Mark and Mary got along like oil and water.

At their first staff meeting, Mark asked for his managers to present a 20-minute briefing on their responsibilities, projects, and performance. Mary, in her stereotypical thinking persona, pulled out all the stops and delivered a 20-minute high-tech PowerPoint presentation complete with animated graphics, transitioning screens, and embedded video as she outlined the myriad of accomplishments and productivity statistics her division achieved in the past year. The last three minutes of her presentation was an analysis of work in progress, complete with milestones and critical elements necessary for future success.

Mark's comments were "But what about your people? What's their morale? Is your turnover less than industry average? How about absenteeism? What were the results of your last employee opinion survey? Who are your best performers? Do you have intact work teams in place? And why did your entire presentation focus only on results and plans? I'm also interested in the soul of your division."

Mary was shocked! From that day forward, Mark sees Mary as a gutsy, but uncaring manager. As long as Mark is her boss, she will probably be passed over for promotion to more responsible positions. It's not Mary's fault, it's Mark's perspective that will hold her back.

Bill, on the other hand, is a senior programmer working in the same company for Kevin. Bill is one of the most popular people in his department, and always has time to listen and empathize with his co-workers. Bill does good work, and although he's not quite as fast as most programmers, he is very thorough and works especially well when coordinating with customers and suppliers.

Kevin, his analytical boss, appreciates the efforts Bill puts into doing a good job, but believes he can be even more productive if he'd cut back on the "social time" he spends during code reviews and delivery milestones with his customers. Bill is in line to be promoted to master programmer in the next six months, but Kevin has his doubts about recommending the promotion. At their last code review, Bill actually suggested they allow the customer to spend a week with him as he debugged the final draft before it was compiled. It was embarrassing for Kevin to decline the suggestion with the customer present in the room. He felt it was absurd to even suggest such a thing!

These two examples demonstrate how thinkers and feelers can find themselves polarized when it comes to decisions about their jobs. This polarization is alive and well in families too.

A family system is much more complex than a business. Traditionally, the man of the house is expected to be the "tougher" member of the partnership and the woman traditionally assumes a care taking and peacekeeper role. The early years of childhood are often experienced in a predominantly feeling world. Tumultuous teenage years later present conflict in the form of statements like "that's not fair" and "you don't care about me"; typical feeling statements of emotions supercharged with hormones.

A four-sided problem solving model addresses the conflict caused by differences in sensing and intuition as well as thinking and feeling. I've discovered it works exceptionally well in families and business alike.

When presented with a situation that requires a decision, first list the details *or* consider the possibilities and the big picture. Your first cut on the decision should be *either* your preference for sensing or intuition. After working the big picture *or* the facts from your preferred perspective, step back and assess them from your *non-preferred* method of gathering data, either sensing or intuition.

Next, analyze your data and develop a potential conclusion or course of action based on your strength in *either* thinking or feeling. After you have a preliminary decision, step back from it once more and consider the implications you might have missed by tapping into your *non-preferred* decision-making style. Let's look at two examples.

You and your family can finally afford to move into a bigger home. Here are the facts:

Sensing
- Affordable house payment
- Four bedrooms and two baths
- Two-car garage
- Nice neighborhood
- Large fenced in yard for Rover

Other possibilities, however, are below.

Intuition
- Save for larger down payment
- Three bedrooms and a finished room over the garage

- Two baths
- One-car garage and rent a room at a storage facility
- Build in the countryside cheaper but a longer commute
- Smaller yard with electronic fence for Rover

The logical conclusion is this thought process:

Thinking

- Build, then close with a variable-rate mortgage
- Four bedrooms with two and a half baths
- One-car garage and a small storage building in the backyard
- Choose a neighborhood near public transportation
- One-third acre lot with an electronic fence in the backyard

The impact on others is as follows:

Feeling...

- If we sell before it's finished, we live in an apartment
- Every child will have their own bedroom, and the young ones might be scared
- The second garage area can be used for storage of bicycles and state boards
- Children will have to change schools and make new friends
- The kids like Rover to stay inside anyway

It's obvious that both data gathering and decision-making styles bring value to the equation. Using all four tools before you reach solid conclusions will make you even more effective and efficient in your life.

The second situation is tougher but true. It happened to a fifteen-year-old daughter of a family I've known for years. Here's how the conversation went.

"What are we going to do now? Her plane lands in three hours. We've never been through anything like this. I thought the drugs were bad, but KIDNAP-PING!!!! Why does she put herself in such dangerous situations?"

"We don't know what's been going on with her, honey. She's obviously hurting inside and needs our love. What should we do now? The police say she can come home after they take her statement. They're meeting us all at the airport. Thank God she's not physically harmed!

"I'd like the police to meet the jerk who kidnapped her too. And as for our daughter, she'd have never been in this situation if she wasn't still using drugs. You know what kind of people are in a drug-using crowd."

"Of course I do. We've been in counseling with her for two years. It seems like she just got psycho-smart rather than healthier."

"I think our only option is in-patient treatment. If she doesn't get off drugs, she will have to leave our home. How can we expose her younger brothers and sisters to that culture? It's only logical that if you have a tumor, you cut it out or get rid of it. If the in-patient treatment can't get rid of the "drug tumor", we'll have to do it ourselves."

"This is our daughter you're treating so cavalierly, my dear. How can you say that?"

"Because our other children cry themselves to sleep every night scared of the bums they see her with. That's how!"

"But it's not only her fault. There must be something we can do to keep the family together. Do we have to send her away? I can cut back to part-time and be home with all the kids every afternoon when school is out."

"That's not the issue, sweetheart. The issue is her drug use and whether or not she's willing to quit them and her drug using friends in order to stay a resident member of our family. It has nothing to do with your job."

"But if she leaves, the children will miss her so much. They love her even though they hate how she's behaved lately. Can't we do something else?"

"You tell me. I'm at my wit's end. I've read two dozen books, seen counselors, ministers, and teachers. I've gone to Alcoholics and Narcotics Anonymous meetings with her. I've stayed up late for her, and even followed her and tapped her phone. What else is there?"

"I don't know, but I don't think causing more pain and suffering by sending her away is the answer."

As you read this conversation, which was near verbatim to the real one, could you see and feel the head and heart in conflict? Both parents love their daughter, and had one of life's toughest decisions to make.

The daughter experienced a miracle. Today, she is clean, sober, and an awesome young lady. She's a role model for many others, and cherished as a gift from God by her family. She is loved. She is also a deviant from statistics. The relapse rate on drug using teens is overwhelming. She's one of the few who have successfully made a commitment to live a new life without drugs.

She and her parents will tell you that the only way they have survived as a family so far is that they made the decision to seek in-patient counseling with both their heads and their hearts. The daughter will tell you that intellectual understanding about the risks of drug use didn't cause her to quit. Neither did the emotional understanding of what she was doing to herself and her family.

She will tell you that it was the marriage of her mind and her heart that gave her the fortitude to quit drugs.

She was a thinker and a feeler on that life-changing issue. Either one alone wasn't strong enough to make work the toughest decision she's ever made.

Her advice to families and teens she counsels is.....

"God gave you a brain and a heart. Neither can function without the other. Use them both when you have to make the *big* decisions in life. And ignore neither on even the little things you do every day. It's hard to do this by accident. You've got to commit to it and be *intentional* to make both parts work together. Take it from one who's been there and almost lost her life and her family. It's worth the effort."

What a kid, huh?

CHAPTER SEVEN

May 17, 1989
McLean, Virginia

Tracy: "This'll be a great job to have. A church in Georgia wants me to spend a week with them to set up their computer systems and teach their staff to use the word processing and financial tracking programs. I've never left the boys with you that long on your own. Do you think you can handle it?"

John: "Sure, Tracy, piece of cake. I'll just be Mr. Mom and Mr. Dad for a week. You go and teach them everything they need to know, and I'll hold down the fort here. No worries."

Tracy: "Great! I knew I could count on you. You know, John, you're a great Dad, but there are a lot of day-to-day things we do that you've never been in charge of before. I've only got four weeks before I have to go to Georgia. Maybe we should start planning now for what you need to do to manage the household and the children by yourself."

John: "We've got plenty of time for that honey. Why don't we wait until a few days before you have to go so it'll be fresh in my mind?"

Tracy: "No, I really think we need to work on it now. There are too many things that might slip through the cracks if you don't plan properly for them."

John: "Come on, Tracy. It's a whole month before you have to go. Do we have to start this now?"

Tracy: "Are you saying you don't think my job at home is important?"

John: "Of course not, honey. I'm just saying that a month is too long to spend planning for a week of routine life at home."

Tracy: "Then you don't think it's important enough to spend a little effort now so you can do the right thing later?"

John: "That's not what I'm saying at all. I just think you're getting pretty worked up about all this planning you think I need to do."

Tracy: "Well, I think that's a pretty irresponsible attitude."

John: "Who are you calling irresponsible?!!"

Tracy: "You, that's who! If you are not going to take this seriously, I'm not so sure I need to be leaving you and the boys alone for a week. Maybe I should just cancel my trip. On second thought, I'm sure I'll cancel the trip. They can just send their staff here."

John: "Talk about irresponsible! You're willing to cancel a new client just because I don't want to spend the next four weeks planning my life down to every minute! How can you live like that?"

Tracy: "I'll tell you how I can live like that! I cover your butt every time you forget something that should have been scheduled all along. I take the kids where they need to be, and they're never late. I make sure they study, eat healthy meals, get enough sleep, play with good friends, go to church with us, and a thousand other things you can't seem to be bothered with! That's how I live like that! You tell me how you can live by the seat your pants!"

John: "I'll tell you how! I don't spend my life worrying about meeting the next deadline or planning every tiny detail that comes along. And who says I live my life by the seat my pants? I earn a good living, provide for you and the boys, do things as a husband and father that lots of other husbands and fathers never get around to, and everyone who meets me would say I'm VERY responsible!"

Tracy: "Well, John, I can see your 'responsible' character isn't revealing itself right now. That's enough. The trip is canceled. You don't have to worry about planning anymore."

John: "That's fine with me! You do what you have to do, and I'll do what I have to do!"

Have you ever noticed how lumpy even a good couch feels at three in the morning? For a week? Experience some form of this conversation with your spouse, and you just might find out.

✲✲✲

To plan or not to plan?

Organizations have institutionalized planning and decision-making for centuries. We've all heard the axioms.

- Plan your work and work your plan.
- Prioritized daily task lists are the key to success.
- If you don't have a destination planned, any path will get you there.
- A person without a plan is often used by a person with one.

Planning and structure in one's life at work is perceived as a valuable trait. This characteristic, actually a personality preference, is measured by the Myers-Briggs Type Indicator on two opposing scales. Judging and Perception.

Someone who has a personality preference of Judging is planned, structured, and organized. They tend to be decisive and approach most of their personal and professional lives with great forethought. A Judger who is forced to respond spontaneously to today's activities is often stressed. People with a strong pre-disposition to planning might even "shut down" when presented with too many options and not enough time to evaluate and plan alternatives.

The opposing preference to Judging is called Perception. A Perceptor is more spontaneous, often indecisive, and prefers to evaluate all the options before making a decision, which usually comes at, near, or even beyond the deadline for action. Perceptors remind me of my next-door neighbor's Boston Terrier, Bruiser.

Bruiser can run out of his back door and charge full speed ahead toward a cat lounging lazily thirty yards away. Halfway there, a squirrel chatters off to the left. Bruiser makes a full-speed left-hand turn toward the squirrel. As he's running, a bird chirps behind him. He stops on a dime, turns around, and races as fast as his squatty little legs will carry him toward the bird, forgetting all about the cat and the squirrel. Halfway to the bird, he hears a whistle that signals a dog biscuit is waiting when he comes back inside. Forgetting about the cat, squirrel, and bird, he races to the door. Exhausted, he drops to the floor and chews on a milk bone, happy to be a dog.

Judgers, on the other hand, remind me of our cat, Splotchy. This twenty-year-old tortoise-shell queen of the house never does anything without a full assessment, evaluation, test, and decision. The only thing that prompts spontaneous behavior on behalf of this stately creature is the sound of running water from the bathroom tap or the electric can opener growling in the kitchen.

Dogs, cats, people, and organizations all share a pre-disposition toward one or the other of these preferences. Recognizing the need for and validity of both preferences in families is an art. I estimate that at two-thirds of the conflict in family relationships can find its roots in the difference between Judging and Perception. Judging words spoken to Perceptors are "irresponsible, seat of the pants, uncaring, and procrastinator." Perceptor words spoken to Judgers are "wound too tight, overbooked fanatic, can't have fun, and over-controlling."

All these words are *destructive*, not *constructive*.

It's important to note that everyone tries on these new behaviors as a child. We lock into a solid preference only as we get older. Most teenagers, regardless of their preference between Judging and Perception, will see a three-week assignment to complete a term paper as having two-and-a-half weeks off. When we reach about twenty years of age, however, and most of us do that with great aplomb, we tend to lock in our preference. We spend the rest of our life placing great value on either Judging or Perception characteristics. Either of these is okay and has its place in life and families. Neither of them should be deemed as inferior to the other.

Understanding your own preference for planning or spontaneity is fairly easy to assess. The Web site www.keirsey.com has a brief version of the Myers-Briggs Type Indicator that could be useful in determining your personality preferences.

Judging is one of the easiest characteristics to observe in other people. Walk around your company and look for the person who has a full-sized Franklin Day Planner filled wall-to-wall with notes, schedules, and activities. Unless it's owned by a person who is masquerading as a closet Perceptor, you will have most likely identified a diehard Judger.

On the other hand, listen for the person who calls a friend

at 11:45 a.m. to ask where she wants to go to lunch. Then, watch how the decision is made. The poor Perceptor just can't seem to make up his mind where to eat until they've considered every option on restaurant row.

Judgers almost always show up for meetings early. Perceptors are observed crashing in at the last-minute, or even a few minutes late, with papers and files in both arms just in case they need to be discussed. Judgers are the last ones to back down when a former decision must be altered. Perceptors are the first to throw numerous options onto the table before any decision might possibly be made. Judgers love decisiveness. Perceptors love options. Judgers value structure. Perceptors value matrix organizations. Judgers embrace rules. Perceptors challenge them.

We all have a preference for one or the other. Now for the "so what."

Can a person with a strong preference toward Judging change? Should a person with a strong preference for Judging change to become a Perceptor? Yes and no, in that order.

Can a person who prefers Perception change? Should this person change to become a Judger? Again, yes and no, in that order.

Should both appreciate and accommodate people with the opposite preference? Absolutely!

It's important to teach our children responsible behaviors. This education includes doing homework and completing their duties and responsibilities on time. It's also important to teach them to allow for pure, unadulterated spontaneity. Both preferences have significant value in family systems. Learning when to invoke either and when to allow for the other is a challenge for parents.

I've seen parents talk until they are blue in the face lecturing their children about homework and chores. It seems that a

Judging parent with a Perceptor child spends about fourteen years repeating the same responsibility lecture over and over. After about three years of lecture, perhaps a new strategy would be in order.

Consequences to behavior cause change. Consequences experienced outside of the family system often cause permanent change. Placing a child on restriction for waiting until the last-minute to complete a report is a family system consequence. Getting an F on that poorly researched report from their teacher *and* being required to do it all again (which can be prompted on the sidelines between the teacher and parent) is an externally imposed consequence.

Missing a birthday party or a Saturday matinee because a child forgot to arrange transportation with the parent is an external consequence. Listening to a responsibility lecture all the way to the theater is a family system consequence.

Being grumpy when the dinner is fish instead of the chicken a child was looking forward to (while making everyone at the table fairly miserable with their lousy attitude) is an attempt on the child's part to force the family to stick to the original dinner plans. Excusing the child from the table so that the family can enjoy their meal in peace is a consequence that might cause the child to think twice the next time things don't go exactly according to plan.

It is very important that parents recognize when children do their best work. Judgers will most often excel at a task when they are given appropriate time and structure to plan and perform their work. Perceptors do their best work when the deadline gets closer. When we make a Judger child wait until the deadline is near before starting a job, report, task, or chore, we will get substandard work and a stressed-out child. When we make a Perceptor child plan, structure, and begin her work far ahead of the deadline, we get the same result. Developing children to allow for their strengths and create alternative behaviors to accommodate the weaknesses of their preferences is the challenge.

Another component of these two preferences is decisiveness. It's fascinating to observe four Judgers and a Perceptor in a restaurant. Watch how they order their food. Judgers typically open their menu, begin reading in the upper left-hand corner, and read down the page until they find exactly what they wish to order. They will then close their menu, lay it aside, and wait for the server. A Perceptor, on the other hand, opens his menu and immediately expresses wonderment at all the options available. He'll pour over every entree, evaluating the pros and cons of each. It's hilarious to watch him poll the table:

"What are you going to have? How about you? What are you going to order? What looks good to you?"

By this time, the Judgers just want to slap some sense into the hapless Perceptor.

When the server arrives to take the orders, the Perceptor encourages the Judgers to order first. Of course, this offer is fine with them. They've already decided on their order. Finally, the spotlight shines squarely on the Perceptor. He'll begin to order, change his mind, and finally commit to something only after hearing the specials enumerated one. . . more. . . time. . . . Of course, substitutions are mandatory.

During the wait for the food to arrive, Perceptors will fret and worry that they should have ordered something different. Don't worry, this display is just natural behavior for a Perceptor, even though it drives Judgers crazy.

Any effective strategy for Judgers who must work or live with Perceptors is to limit the number of options available. Judgers can "plan" their behavior and activities with a Perceptor by agreeing to accept any one of two or three options. This plan minimizes the time it takes for a Perceptor to consider the possibilities and adds a small modicum of structure for a Judger to hang onto.

The "hit and run" style works well when one finds it necessary to encourage a Judger to change a plan or consider other options. Here's how it works with Judgers and Perceptors who don't value the opposite preference in their personalities.

Sunday, 12:15 p.m.
Driving home from church

Husband: "Let's go out to lunch today."

Wife: "No."

Husband: "Why?"

Wife: "Because I have something already planned for lunch."

Husband: "Let's have that for dinner tomorrow night. I feel like going out for lunch today."

Wife: "Personally, I think it is irresponsible for you even to suggest we go to lunch now."

Husband: "What do you mean irresponsible?"

Wife: "Didn't you just tell me that cash flow stinks this month, Jimmy has a birthday party to go to at 3:00, and the lines are out the doors at every restaurant in town by now. Don't you think about these things before you come up with these wild ideas at the last minute?"

Husband: "Alright already, let's just go home."

The ride home is tense and silent, and lunch is a social disaster. Now let's look at how a "Hit and Run" might have changed that Sunday afternoon.

Sunday, 10:00 a.m.
Walking into church

Husband: "I'm thinking about going out to lunch today, honey. Think about it, and we'll talk after church."

Sunday, 12:15 p.m.
Driving home from church

Wife: "Let's go! If we're going out to lunch like you want, we'd better get a move on. We'll save 20 minutes if we can beat the Presbyterian congregation there."

The "hit and run" technique simply allows Judgers time to adjust their plans to include new activities. A side benefit is fairly obvious.

One of the ways that a Judger changes a plan is by moaning, groaning, griping, and complaining while he rearranges already scheduled activities so that he can accommodate something new. This behavior is often taken personally by someone caught in their crosshairs. It shouldn't be. It's simply the nature of the way Judger changes plans. The "Hit and Run" technique gives Judgers the space they need to change their plans. The person encouraging the change, whether it is another Judger or a Perceptor, doesn't have to listen to all the negative chatter while a *new* plan is being constructed.

Naturally, a prerequisite to using this technique effectively is that Perceptors must "plan their spontaneity" to a certain degree to accommodate Judgers' structured nature.

Nearly everyone in a family relationship experiences conflict from time to time. Much of this conflict derives from the planning and decisiveness versus the flexible and spontaneous personality preferences. Understanding, appreciating, and accommodating people with preferences different than your own are marks of maturity and collaboration.

A number of years ago, I was explaining this concept to a group of thirty-five civil servants, using the letters "J" and "P" to refer to Judgers and Perceptors. After telling some really funny stories about my family and friends and our different perspectives on life, I told the story about Tracy and John disagreeing on the need to plan his week during her absence. Here is the moral of the story:

> After studying the differences in their personalities and preferences, John now understands Tracy's J'ness and she now appreciates his P'ness. (Go ahead, say it out loud, and hold on to the arms of your chair to keep from falling out.) I, being the Perceptor that I am and having never said that line before, didn't understand why the entire room burst into raucous laughter.
>
> Even though it's true, (as it's written, and maybe even spoken, who knows?), you can believe I choose my words much more carefully today. Having experienced the embarrassing consequence of speaking without planning, I'm convinced that having at least some Judging tendencies is not a bad thing at all.

CHAPTER EIGHT

A conversation between a mother and her son, Sean.

Mother: "What a great day, Sean. Your first day in Little League. We've got the camera all set, slugger!"

Sean: "I can't wait! I'm going to buy you and Dad the biggest house and the best car in the world when I'm drafted by the Padres. You just wait, Mom, I'll make the All Stars my first year!"

Two weeks later...

Sean: "I don't want to go to practice, Mom. Everybody laughs at me. I can't hit the ball, grounders go between my legs half the time, and I dropped three fly balls in right field last week. Can I just stay home today? My stomach hurts."

Three weeks later...

Sean: "Did you see it Mom! It would have been a home run if I hadn't caught it at the fence. Man, was I nervous. The ball must have gone a mile up in the sky. I was afraid I'd drop it and everyone would laugh at me, and I almost did when the lights got in my eyes from the corner of right field. I'm glad it wasn't a line drive. I still duck every time one comes my way. I wish I played as good as David. He doesn't even flinch at shortstop."

Three months later...

Sean: "Mom! I made it! I'm an All Star! We start practice next week. I think I'm going to play right field, but that's okay. I'm getting better every time I play. Do you think you or Dad could hit a few line drives to me? I could use the practice."

That afternoon...

Sean: "Hit it harder Mom. That's not a line drive. It's more like a dribble to the pitcher."

Sean: "That's better, Mom. Swing level. You can do it. You're hitting it harder and harder every time. See, you didn't need to go back inside. You just needed a little more practice. It's fun to do this together."

Sean: "Wow, Mom. Go a little easier on it, how about it? You hit that one into the Johnsons' yard. Where'd you get muscles like that?"

The next day...

Sean: "It'll be okay, Mom. I know how to do this. I've seen you and Dad do it a million times. How hard can backing out of the driveway be, anyway? I can do it. Let me press the pedals. You look out of the mirror. Okay, it's in reverse. I'll go slowly. Come on, Mom! Take your hand off of the steering wheel. Wait until I tell my friends at school that I can drive!"

From the lap of his mother in the driver's seat, ten-year-old Sean generates sounds heard around the neighborhood. Screech, squeal, bump, pedal-to-the-metal, engine-racing-heart-stopping-RPMs concluding with a resounding crash that transforms their mailbox into a stump.

Sean was ready to play baseball. He did well at school. He was prepared to ride a bicycle, do his homework, make his bed, feed himself, walk, talk, and generally manage his ten-year-old existence with efficiency and effectiveness.

But he was not ready to drive.

✿✿✿

I Can Do It, Maybe

Think about your first day on your new job. You probably cleaned up nicely that day, wore your best clothes, got a haircut, plastered a smile on your face, and consciously offered firm handshakes with solid eye contact to everyone you met. Of course, a good impression was important on your first day. You were excited, confident, and ready to take on the world.

You didn't even know where the bathroom was.

After orientation, which often consists of an introduction to your workspace, memorization of your phone number, signing a zillion forms and acquiring an ID badge, you made your way to your small part of corporate real estate that would contain your future efforts in the organization. In other words, you found your desk.

At home that night, you offered a recital of the day's sojourn, which was less enchanting than you had expected. In fact, it was probably a pretty boring day. Chin up, however, because after all, it was just your first day. Day number two of your reign was yet to unfold.

Around day number fourteen, you were probably asking yourself what the heck you had gotten yourself into. You had yet to master the computer system. The idiosyncrasies of e-mail and voice jail were still a mystery. Everybody seemed to have advice about who to trust and who to avoid. Your boss probably spent most of her time in meetings instead of working with you. And to top it all off, you inadvertently set off the alarm last night after you left the building. In your heart of hearts, this job wasn't all it was cracked up to be.

After a few months, however, you were getting better at corporate survival skills. Your work was acceptable, and you'd even prepared a few presentations for the Quality Committee about your most recent project. Things seemed to be settling in, but you still weren't accepted on equal ground with everyone else. Occasionally, you asked stupid questions, and in moments of serious brain gas, you forged ahead on your own only to discover that you should have been asking more stupid questions.

Today is a big day. You're celebrating your first anniversary of employment, and you feel good about what you've accomplished this past year. You are an organizational lean, mean, production machine. On Monday, you're in charge of bringing in a newbie to the company. There's a pool in the office betting on whether the fresh meat will be wearing spit-shined shoes and a new tie.

Mike, your friend in the next cube, has inserted a hidden computer program on the newbie's hard drive. As soon as he touches any key, the program will make the computer act like a washing machine, and for about thirty seconds will wash, spin, and clean the hard drive, complete with washing machine sound effects while draining cyber-water from the keyboard.

It'll Be a Great Monday

These scenarios describe a concept known as Situational Leadership® II development levels. There are two components in a development level. Competence and commitment.

Competence is defined as task-relevant knowledge and skills and transferable skills. Task-relevant knowledge and skills is the ability to perform a *specific* task. Transferable skills are similar skills you might possess that parallel the duties necessary to perform a task. For example, if the task is to use Microsoft's Word for Windows, a person who has never used that program might bring significant transferable skills if they have experience using WordPerfect for Windows.

Commitment is defined as motivation and confidence. Motivation is a person's enthusiasm for a task. Confidence is a person's feeling of being able to perform that task well alone. These two things describe your "Attitude" about a task.

Combining competence and commitment at a particular task creates a person's development level. It is important to understand that a person can be many different development levels at the same time. Development levels apply to a specific task, not to a person. I might be very competent, motivated, and confident that I can operate my automobile in rush hour traffic. However, I might be unsure, unmotivated, and incompetent at operating a heavy tractor trailer rig in the same conditions. In this case, I might have one development level for automobile tasks and a totally different development level for tractor trailer rigs, even in the same driving conditions. To illustrate the difference in development levels, I'll describe three situations.

First, lets look at something near and dear to my heart. In South Carolina, we have a really stupid law stating that when a child turns fifteen, with parental consent, that munchkin may go to the Department of Motor Vehicles and seek a daytime permit to drive a killing machine on the state's highways and byways.

My daughter, Megan, in her fifteenth year of existence, convinced us that she should acquire the privilege of doing just that. That Friday afternoon, she came running out of the DMV waving her newly minted permit in the air explaining, "Dad, Dad, I passed the test. Let me drive! I'm ready!"

Seated behind the wheel of my ancient Toyota Celica with a five-speed transmission and bucket seats, she prepared to embark upon her journey to freedom. She actually turned to me even before inserting the key into the ignition and asked, "Dad, can I borrow the car this weekend?"

At that moment in time, Megan had dippidy-doo-da competence at driving, but motivation and confidence that barely stayed on the scale of commitment. In the South, we call that "Squat for Skills." My title for this development level is "Blithering Idiot with a Great Attitude."

Two weeks later, she had run over three trash cans and two mailboxes. Mothers would bring their children off the street when she opened the driver's side door. Dogs and cats sought refuge behind bushes and trees when the Celica's engine raced in my driveway. Driving was an embarrassment to Megan.

Of course, she could crank it up, put on her seat belt, operate the turn signals, and occasionally sequence through the gears. Accelerating, however, was akin to riding a roller coaster named "Thunder Guts" over steroid-enhanced speed bumps. For Megan, synchronizing the clutch and gas remained one of life's unsolved mysteries. Her friends were asking her when she could start driving to school, and she was about ready to throw her hands in the air and buy an annual pass on the metro bus line. Expectations and reality passed like two ships in the night.

She was firmly entrenched in the next development level, number two.

Over the next few months, her skills continually improved. She did a fairly good job at driving in normal conditions, but her knuckles turned inexplicably white and her heart raced wildly every time she had to pass on a two-lane road. Merging in the rain onto the interstate at sixty miles per hour with eighteen wheelers dancing on their air horns invoked not anger, but fear. For the most part, she had mastered the basic skills of driving. Her confidence at performing the more difficult tasks was her new challenge.

The third development level had been acquired.

Today, many years later, she is a superb driver. She has a spotless driving record and manipulates her Saturn Vue with aplomb on the thoroughfares of South Carolina. In fact, her competence and commitment are so firm that they are almost hidden from the view of others. At the task of driving, she has arrived at development level four.

These four development levels are distinctly different from one another.

Another way of thinking about these four development levels is to imagine the levels of skill and consciousness about that skill. Persons at a development level one are unconsciously unskilled. They don't even know what they don't know. They're just glad to be there. This condition mirrors yours on your first day at work, your first day in little league, your first computer upon opening the box, and a million of life's challenges when first presented.

A person at development level two is consciously unskilled. Now you know what you don't know, and it's depressing. Not only are you unskilled at the task, but your attitude (motivation and confidence) stinks. It's a lousy place to be, albeit perfectly normal. It's an even lousier place to stay, which is exactly what happens to many people as they decide to quit a task.

At development level three, you are consciously skilled. You know what to do, but you have to think about it. You can see this when using a computer. If you're proficient and confident at using a mouse (a development level four) try to use someone else's trackball, or a pointer stick on a laptop. You might not have to think about using a mouse, but you will find the need to concentrate on making the cursor perform with a trackball.

At development level four, you're unconsciously skilled, like when you are using a mouse on your own computer. You're probably a development level four at driving, eating, walking, using a phone, and a myriad of other life tasks we do daily. Doing them without thinking about them makes you qualified to be at this level.

This rather academic study of a person's competence and commitment has been well defined since the days of the Cave Man.

Development Level One

Little Matilda, at about twelve months old, stood excitedly in her jail cell, (we call them cribs, but from the inside they look exactly like prison bars) and concluded that there was a better way to propel herself around the world than to continue motoring about on all fours. Consequently, with Mom or Dad providing a captivated audience, she took her first step. Applause erupted, congratulations were offered (in baby-talk, of course) and the obligatory grandparent notification message about Matilda's first step was accomplished. Matilda, at that point in life, had the skill to take only one step but was excited about this newfound method of propulsion.

Development Level Two

Garnering all of her strength and courage, she soon progressed to the next stage of development. Basking in the celebration of her first step, she attempted to transfer her weight from back to front foot while shifting forward, completing an often observed formula for her second step. She abruptly found herself sitting squarely on her behind while tears pooled in both eyes and a disquieting scream emerged from her lips. At this development level, she has enough skill to take one step but not two, and her confidence and motivation have been shattered, as evidenced by her tears and crying.

Development Level Three

A mysterious phenomenon occurs in most children when they reach the age of two. They forget how to walk. Running is king. With uncanny predictability, most households with a two-year old in residence will experience something similar at least weekly. Matilda, loitering around the kitchen observing lunchtime preparations, is enlightened with a magnificent thought that she should do something incredibly interesting in her bedroom. It's not much different from watching the GE Light Bulb commercial. Her eyes light up, a mischievous grin appears on her face, and she boldly races on ballerina tiptoes out of the kitchen, through the dining area, past the living room, and while making the turn to go down the hall or up the stairs, her little tractionless toes fail her and propel her body firmly into the wall or against the steps. Again, as it was with the second step she attempted and failed a year ago, she starts to cry.

She is a master at walking, but has a few things to learn about maneuvering around curves. Her competence is fairly high, but the waterfall of tears coupled with the ear-piercing siren emulating from her lips is a dead giveaway that her motivation and confidence are less than stellar. Welcome, Matilda, to the third development level.

Development Level Four

As any parent of a fifteen-year-old teenager will testify, she needs very little instruction or encouragement about walking while blazing through her teenage years. Driving, however, is a completely different story. Her pedantic efforts at physical propulsion demonstrate exceptional competence and commitment, but her newfound freedom behind the wheel of the family car accelerates the acquisition of gray hair for her parents.

At walking, Matilda has achieved the fourth development level—high competence and commitment. Driving is another story. At that task, she is somewhere else on the development continuum.

Kathy, my beautiful and incredibly intelligent wife, approached me about fifteen years ago with a request to teach her to use a word processing program on our computer. Being the unashamed techno-geek that I am, I scheduled our first lesson.

Having no competence but great enthusiasm to learn this skill, she was my affectionately labeled "Blithering Idiot with a Great Attitude."

After teaching her how to start the program, manipulate the mouse, and the basics of computer typing, such as word wrap and the arrow keys, I felt really good about myself. The next day, she sat down while all alone to type a letter to her sister. In a record two minutes and 37 seconds flat, she locked up the keyboard to the point that the only alternative was to invoke the powers of the Very Big Red Button (VBRB). She called my office and frantically asked if she had lost anything important or hurt the computer (they feel no pain, honestly). During that brief conversation, she swore off computers for the rest of her life. The second level of development had reared its ugly head.

After much prodding and cajoling, she spent the next few months learning the basics of both word processing and computers. She was actually doing quite well until she decided to publish a newsletter for the youth of our church. Formatting columns became her nemesis.

In yet another phone call she expressed her confusion and frustration at managing widows and orphans in a three column landscape document. Fifteen minutes later, she hung up with the basic knowledge of this function and was armed with a few handwritten notes and the word processing manual. She was firmly entrenched in the third stage of development, possessing most of the competence she needed to perform the task, but only moderate motivation and confidence that she could do it all alone from start to finish.

Today, Kathy works with churches that use computers to automate many of their administrative functions. She knows her way around both hardware and software, and truly enjoys working in this field. To her customers and in her own heart, she is both competent and committed, the fourth development level.

Less than I percent of managers in organizations are proficient at providing appropriate types of leadership to all four development levels. I suspect the same results would be revealed in families.

Once development levels are accurately assessed, you're halfway home. Your response to each development level describes your leadership style. The definition of leadership style is the pattern of behaviors you use to influence others as perceived by them. Two distinctly different behaviors comprise your leadership style. Read on.

CHAPTER NINE

Do any of these family conversations sound familiar to you?

Husband: "Great, sweetheart. This'll be a really neat thing for you to learn. I use computers and can teach you in no time at all. You're a really bright person. You graduated at the top of your class in high school and college, and I know you'll have no trouble at all learning this. What do you think you should learn first?"

Wife: "I don't know. Can I hurt it?"

Husband: "No, you can't hurt it. But that was a good question. You see, you're perceptive when it comes to computers. I've been thinking about what to teach you first, but I'm interested in using your ideas about how to do it instead of just telling you what to do. What do you think we should do first?"

Wife: "Maybe you should just tell me what to do."

Husband: "No, no, no! You can figure it out. Think about it, sweetheart. How do you want to go about learning to use word processing?"

Wife: "Okay, you asked for it. *What buttons do I punch to word process?*"

✿✿✿

Mother: "I'll be in the living room if you need any help, honey. I know this is the first time you've cooked spaghetti, but you've watched me do it a hundred times. You just call me if you have any problems."

Son: "But Mom, I don't know how to do it."

Mother: "That's okay. It'll come to you as soon as you get started. Why don't you brown the hamburger first and then just do what you think needs to be done next. Call me if you need any help."

Son: "Mom! I don't know how to do it."

Mother: "You'll figure it out sweetheart it's not hard at all."

***

Father: "No, you cannot go with your friends to the movie tonight."

Daughter: "But Dad, I've done all my chores, and my room is clean. My homework is done for the weekend, and I've even helped Mom do the dishes. Please, can I go out with Amy and Carol?"

Father: "You heard me the first time. You should've talked with me about this earlier if you wanted permission to go out tonight."

Daughter: "Dad! Please!"

Father: "If you put your feet under my table and live under my roof, young lady, you'll do exactly what I say when I say it. Now go practice your piano, and don't let me hear another word about it. I'll tell you when you can go out."

***

Son: "Mom tells me you're thinking about buying a new car. I think that's great, Dad. You've been driving that old battle-wagon since I was a teenager. What are you thinking about buying?"

Father: "Well, son, I was thinking about one of those minivans. They've got lots of room and should be great to drive to the mountains in the fall."

Son: "That's an option, Dad, but I think you should get something a little more practical since it's just you and Mom at home now. How about a mid-sized Buick?"

Father: "We've been driving a Buick for decades. I think I'm ready for a change. I kind of like the idea of sitting in a cockpit and cruising the highway."

Son: "That might be fun for a while, but a vehicle like that is too much for you and Mom to handle around town. You should think seriously about buying another Buick."

Father: "I don't think you're listening, son. Now that you kids are up and gone, your Mom and I are ready for a little change of pace. Besides, I've got about fifty years of driving experience under my belt. I wasn't really asking for your opinion, you know."

Son: "You're a big boy, Dad, but you're making a big mistake getting a minivan. You should listen to me. A Buick is the best bet at your age."

Father: "My age has nothing to do with it. And you're acting like a fifteen-year-old know-it-all. Your Mom and I are perfectly capable of making this decision on our own."

Son: "Okay, okay. But don't complain to me when you figure out that you have more car than you want or need. I think I know best in this situation what you and Mom should do."

✱✱✱

Where Do I Stand With You?

The second component of Situational Leadership® II is your response to a person's development level. Your response is composed of a mixture of directive and supportive behaviors.

Directive behavior includes telling and showing someone what to do. You are using directive behavior when you set goals, outline action steps, list instructions, give orders, and enumerate specifications that should be observed. Directive behavior is not a bad thing. Many people shy away from it because they think it is over-controlling or belittling. Not so, if it's used in the right circumstances.

Supportive behavior includes giving feedback, asking questions, encouraging, facilitating, involving the person in the decision-making process, and generally being nice. Most people see supportive behavior as a pleasant and effective demonstration of their leadership style. This belief is an accurate assessment only when supportive behavior is used at the correct time.

The first style of leadership is a mixture of high direction and low support. At Parris Island, South Carolina, we have a military installation devoted to training young men and women to become Marines. The wonderful person who meets new recruits as they exit the bus will use this style of leadership, especially in the beginning of the boot camp experience. This method is also the style one might use in an emergency or crisis.

The second style of leadership is a mixture of high direction and high support. You see this most often on the baseball field at Little League practice. When newcomer Johnny dribbles his first-ever hit halfway down the first base line, his coach will praise his progress, direct him on his stance and swinging technique, smile, and encourage him to hit the next one even harder.

The third style of leadership significantly reduces directive behavior while maintaining high supportive behavior. This style is most often used by counselors, ministers, psychiatrists, and psychologists. Their conversations include many questions, facilitation of activities, and encouragement. They do not often tell someone what to do without first getting input from them.

The fourth and final style of leadership uses very little directive or supportive behavior. This form is the style of leadership that most parents use with their children upon leaving home for college or as they embark upon their adult life. This style is most effectively used when people know what to do and how to do it as well as having a good attitude about performing a task.

Caterpillar's Track Type Tractors division uses this leadership model as a way of demonstrating their values. When a manager chooses to use a style of leadership that supports the development level of her people on specific tasks, it is considered a way of demonstrating trust, respect, empowerment, and teamwork, the company's top four values. Knowing how to use each style is only half of the equation. Knowing *when* to use it is just as important.

The formula is straightforward. When a person *does not* have competence at a task, you should use high direction. When they *do* have competence, you allow them to provide their own direction. When a person *does not* have commitment at a task, you should use high support. When they *do* have commitment, you allow them to provide their own support.

The styles of leadership have numbers just like the development levels. Style One is high on direction and low on support,

which corresponds to the low competence and high commitment of a Development Level One. The four styles include these
mixtures of Direction and Support.

1. Development Level One needs Style One, which is
   High Direction and Low Support
2. Development Level Two needs Style Two, which is
   High Direction and High Support
3. Development Level Three needs Style Three, which is
   Low Direction and High Support
4. Development Level Four needs Style Four, which is
   Low Direction and Low Support

This twofold process of diagnosis of development level
and application of leadership style has been used in families for
centuries. We teach children to walk using this technique. The
child who can only stand will come to the outstretched alarms
of Mom or Dad when one is kneeling just a step away (Style
One).

The child with enough skill to take one step, but not two,
is treated to encouragement, praise, and additional direction to
take that second step (Style Two).

The little angel who has slammed against the wall or step
is held and checked for blood or broken bones and quieted with
a soft touch. This child doesn't get a lot of additional direction
on walking, but instead gets sufficient support to bolster his
commitment level (Style Three).

The teenager who walks and runs well gets little direction or support on the topic. Driving, or centuries ago, chariot
racing, brings with it much more direction and support (Style
Four).

Two common parenting styles come to mind when we consider leadership behaviors. The first is the "Drill Sergeant" style
in which a parent uses high direction and low support consis-

tently throughout a child's life. We've all heard of, (or perhaps, experienced) parents who make all the decisions and provide all the instructions for a child on every aspect of his life. These children, upon leaving home, most often score below national norms on nearly every socio-economic scale measurable. The reason is quite simple.

The child who has experienced a highly directive style of parenting has never been challenged to make serious, life-changing decisions on his or her own. Consequently, when they do get out on their own, the quality of their life changing decisions is less than that of a child whose parents have trained her to make good decisions.

Another, parenting style is the "Firefighter." This parent uses low direction and high support. Firefighters make lots of noise, charge through dangerous places, and rescue people from the clutches of disaster. Firefighter parents do the same thing. These are the Moms and Dads you'll find in nearly every elementary school in the nation at lunchtime, bringing little Johnny or Lucy his or her lunch that was left on the counter, or delivering the homework which was found on the bed. These are the parents who argue for twelve years with their child's teachers or are constantly calling the coach about why their child isn't playing as much as she should.

Just like the children of a Drill Sergeant, these children grow up to rank lower than their peers, but for a different reason. Children of firefighters have never had to suffer the consequences of their actions because their parents rescued them before the consequence had to be paid. Unfortunately, these children often suffer consequences later in life that are of an adult magnitude rather than a child magnitude. A child who misses a movie, forgoes a lunch, or makes a zero on a homework paper understands that his behavior has a result in his own real life. These results eventually evolve into lost jobs, broken or destructive relationships, and substance abuse if they are first experienced as an adult.

Parenting isn't the only place that leadership plays a role. Try being overly directive with your spouse when she's behind the wheel of the family car. You're sure to get an ear full of mismatched consequences. Attempt to tell your next-door neighbor exactly what pattern to use when cutting his grass. You're sure to alienate your neighbor. Try being supportive and encouraging without giving any instruction the next time someone asks you for directions. Frustration and confusion will abound.

My wife, Kathy, has come up with a great way to *visualize* her leadership style. She sees her style with respect to her physical position while standing with our children.

When our children were small, she made a conscious decision to intervene on their behalf when they were confronted with adult situations or had to collaborate with adults on serious issues about their life, such as practice schedules, school programs, church activities, or controversial situations. In these circumstances, she would stand "in front" of our children, leading the way and making the decisions (Style One).

As our children began to gain some proficiency at specific tasks, she would "stand beside" them on that task. If she were being directive and supportive, she was holding their hands as she walked half a pace in front of them, leading them and encouraging their progress (Style Two). If she were being mostly supportive, she was holding their hands as she walked half a pace behind them, allowing them to lead her while being encouraged in their accomplishments (Style Three).

When our children mastered specific tasks and maintained both motivation and confidence, she would provide low direction and support, which was the equivalent of "standing behind" them (Style Four). In this position, she was not actively directing or supporting them but merely staying nearby to "catch" them should they falter.

This concept of matching your leadership style to someone else's development level allows the other person to develop her skills and solidify her confidence and motivation. A few interesting components of leadership style and its collaboration with development level can be observed. First, rarely do people actually lose competence *unless* they do not practice a specific skill.

For example, I play the piano. Many years ago, I played a song called Chopin's "Revolutionary Etude," or "Etude in C Minor." When I was in college, it was a great way to meet girls, since very few Southern college boys played classical piano. Today, having celebrated the nineteenth anniversary of my twenty-ninth birthday, and having been married for fifty-six years (twenty-eight for Kathy and twenty-eight for me), I can truthfully say that it has been more than two decades since I tickled the ivories with that particular song.

I would venture to say, however, that I could learn to play that song much more quickly than someone who has never played the piano before. Of course, I've got the basic skills down cold, as compared to someone who must first learn to read music and play "Mary Had a Little Lamb" before he graduates to Chopin. My needs at playing the piano are much different than my needs at learning to scan, modify, and fax pictures of my family over the Internet. At piano playing, I need only a little encouragement and about a month of practice. At faxing and scanning, I need someone to tell me exactly what to do and walk me through the process. Understanding someone's needs at each development level is an important part of your leadership style. If a person has been competent at a particular task at some point in her past, her needs may be much different than someone who has never attempted that task before.

Another interesting component of development levels is the difference between the second and the third level. The major difference is not commitment, but competence. When a person reaches the second stage of development, our most common response is to be encouraging and facilitating. This support, however, is *not* alone what is needed.

The Little League baseball player who is crying and wants to quit after two weeks of embarrassing practice needs his coach to teach him how to catch a ground ball, bunt, or field a fly ball. He doesn't need a lot of encouragement as much as he needs significant instruction on minor skills of the game. In other words, accomplishment moves people on the development continuum, especially between the second and third stages.

To be effective at parenting and family leadership, you should have all four styles in your repertoire of behavior. Your high directive and low supportive style should be one that gives clear instruction, specific goals, and attainable performance milestones. When you add supportive behaviors, you should include praise, encouragement, and involvement. The supportive behaviors should be magnified while directive behaviors are minimized when you move to the third style of leadership. Finally, learning to let go and trust someone's competence and commitment on a task that is important to you is frightening. Just ask any parents who have ever driven off campus leaving their little darling behind in a freshmen dormitory room.

As is the theme of many chapters in this book, being *intentional* is paramount to effective and efficient leadership. I spent many years leading my family from the seat of my pants, doing what felt right in my gut at the time. Ken Blanchard and a multitude of people who have been my tutors on these things have convinced me that great leadership doesn't happen by accident. Greatness leading your family is both *situational* and *intentional*.

CHAPTER TEN

Husband: "Can you believe it? One minute we're on our way to a twenty-year Air Force career and the next minute I'm unemployed. What a great wedding present!"

Wife: "It's okay, sweetheart. We'll figure something out. I think it's kind of exciting being newlyweds and starting a new career all at the same time."

Husband: "Well, I'm not very excited! We've got come up with a plan in a hurry, or my name will be mud in your family forever."

Wife: "It's not that bad, honey. You can find a job anywhere."

Husband: "I don't think so. With Vietnam just closing down and a million soldiers and sailors in the job market, I'll be lucky to get a job as a sales clerk in the mall."

One week later...

Husband: "Guess what. I got the job as a part-time sales clerk at the tuxedo store in the mall. I think I'll go back to school and get an M.B.A. at night. I could use it if I'm going into business instead of being a fly-boy."

One year later...

Husband: "Wow, I've never made this much money before. Thirteen thousand dollars goes a long way in South Carolina as long as Jimmy Carter doesn't start a recession for us. I still want to go back to school for that M.B.A., though."

Five years later...

Husband: "I love Charleston. Being the first training manager for the South Carolina State Ports Authority is a fantastic opportunity. I can go back to school and get my M.B.A. now."

Two years later...

Husband: "I guess the only thing we can do is start our own business doing training classes wherever I can pick up a contract. Recessions stink, and training is always the first thing to go. I haven't been unemployed for more than a week since I was fourteen.... I really need that M.B.A. more than ever now."

Three years later...

Husband: "Running two businesses and managing a half dozen employees is driving me crazy. These fourteen-hour days are killing our love life. I don't know how I'll find the time to do all of this and get an M.B.A. too."

Two years later...

Husband: "Okay, this is it. I've been so confident that I could get an M.B.A. that I haven't bothered to get started on it for the last fifteen years. Here's the deal, sweetheart. I'm going back to school at night, get my M.B.A., graduate with a 4.0 average at the top of the class, and do the whole thing in fifteen months. I'll graduate next spring. Mark my words, I'm serious this time."

Fifteen months later...

The room filled with my name, "Ray Alan Snyder." After all those years of talking about getting my advanced degree with my wife Kathy, I finally walked across the stage and was "hooded" by the Dean of the School of Business. It felt good.

The previous fifteen months of my life had been the busiest and most energetic through which I had ever lived. My dad asked, "What made you go back to school this late in life and do so well, son?"

My response was, "Dad, for the first time in fifteen years I put a deadline on that goal. What I thought was a goal set back in 1975 was only a dream. What made things start to happen was the deadline. It caused me to solidify my goal."

✿✿✿

Solidify

Los Angeles Times, January 2, 1998
Goal-setting Goal Eluding 'Reinvented' U.S. Agencies
"The Agriculture Department has set a goal of resolving the problem expected to derail its computers when the calendar year reaches the year 2000— but it does not expect to have its plan ready until 2002."

Organizations have been preaching the merits of goal setting for generations. I remember viewing a training movie in high school in the 1960s that stressed the importance of setting goals for ourselves as we grew into adults. While in the Air Force and Army Reserve, my leadership training was heavily focused on the value of goal setting for my people and myself.

Corporate leadership training programs all include a module or two on the subject. Many include processes, acronyms, step-by-step procedures, and motivational videos that encourage participants to take goal setting seriously.

Nearly all performance management systems worldwide share goal setting as a foundation. Most people have heard the Chinese proverb, "If you don't have a destination, any path will get you there."

Why is it, then, that so many goals are nothing more than dreams and wishes? Perhaps, the fault lies in the formula. As a memory jogger to ensure that all the buttons are punched when setting goals, I use the acronym SOLIDFY. It stands for...

- Specific
- Obstacles
- Liaisons
- Information
- Deadline
- Intrinsic
- Feasible
- Yardlines

This concept is a life skill to teach your children. When all eight SOLIDIFY bases are touched, people find that their energy and activities stay closely focused to those things they've identified as important. In business, we call this performance management. In families, we call it life.

When you find yourself or others in need of direction, goal setting is often the place to start. It makes no difference whether you are working with a three-year-old learning to tie her shoes or a research physicist creating encrypted downlink telemetry for satellite communication systems; these eight steps to setting goals make the task clearer.

Specific

Los Angeles Times, January 2, 1998

Goal-setting Goal Eluding 'Reinvented' U.S. Agencies

"The goals, for the most part, are hardly startling. The statement for the National Weather Service, for example, says it exists to forecast the weather."

Any goal starts out with a degree of specificity that can be articulated in writing. Going back to college is not specific. Getting an M.B.A. is. Making lots of money is not. Increasing your salary by 10 percent is. Learning to dress yourself is not. Learning to button buttons and tie shoes is. Straightening your room is not specific. Making your bed, vacuuming, folding and putting away clothes, and emptying your trashcan are specific.

Kathy and I fought this last example with our daughter Megan for years. As every good parent knows, the order "Clean up your room!" spoken with great authority while implying "or else" is standard fare between teenagers and their domestic rulers. After periodically voicing this command, our expectation was that the room would magically transform itself into a pristine habitat worthy of Martha Stewart's praise and adulation.

To Megan, however, that edict simply meant that she should clear a path from the door to her bed sometime in the ensuing week.

After much frustration and gnashing of teeth, we began to get more specific about our expectations. Were we successful? That question is relevant. Her abode has enjoyed a more presentable appearance in the past few years, but the caverns of her closet and the dark spaces beneath her bed are inexplicably stuffed to capacity.

I guess we weren't always specific enough.

Obstacles

Los Angeles Times, January 2, 1998

Goal-setting Goal Eluding 'Reinvented' U.S. Agencies

"When Clinton ran for President in 1992, he and his running mate, Sen. Al Gore, vowed to 'reinvent government'—that is, to overhaul every department and agency and make it come up with specific long-term goals against which its progress could be judged. An early review by the Government Accounting Office suggests that government's myriad parts and departments may have some work to do before Clinton can readily claim that they have been 'reinvented.'"

Much to our chagrin, we are faced with obstacles of every size and shape when we try to do something important. These roadblocks come in many different flavors.

Obstacles may be people, places, things, or even thoughts. Getting a spouse to "buy-in" to your goal of getting the newest BMW Cruiser Cycle may be an obstacle to reaching your goal, (which, by the way, is a perfectly reasonable goal if it's like the one straddled by James Bond in *Tomorrow Never Dies*). Finding a mentor for your post-graduate research on large-group communication patterns may be a roadblock if you live in a small town. Finding time may hold you back. Finding money may rein in your ambitions.

Perhaps the most inspiring models of overcoming adversity are people with physical challenges that most people consider incapacitating. The list is long, and includes physically incapacitated Stephen Hawking, quadriplegic Christopher Reeves, blind Stevie Wonder, and Heather Whitestone, a near-deaf Miss America. All of them have accomplished incredible feats, and every single one did it with his or her mind wide open to the obstacles they had to meet. These people did not ignore their obstacles, but addressed them head-on to overcome or compensate for them.

I see so many people approach goal setting without considering the obstacles, only to be "slam-dunked" when they are blindsided by them. It is discouraging to go back to college twenty years after your high school graduation only to discover you are woefully unprepared in algebra. It can cause you to become frustrated and possibly abandon your goal should you run out of money halfway through restoration of your kitchen. It is disheartening to a child who wants to quit piano three months into the lessons because he can't quite master the finger exercise on chromatic scales.

Obstacles should be identified and addressed *up-front* in the goal setting process. This is *not* negative thinking, but proactive planning! Foregoing the anticipation of obstacles until you actually bump into them can cause you to modify seriously or even to abandon the goal. I equate this method with the stereotypical ostrich, which buries its head in the sand when trouble appears, thinking that if it can't see itself, then neither can anything else.

Just remember which part of the ostrich's anatomy is exposed when that happens.

Liaisons

Los Angeles Times, January 2, 1998

Goal-setting Goal Eluding 'Reinvented' U.S. Agencies

"The draft plans submitted by the Department of Health and Human Services did not address the question of how to coordinate its alcohol and drug abuse treatment programs, even though they exist in tandem with those of fifteen other federal agencies."

From childhood, we've been taught to be independent and self-sufficient. Goal setting, however, rarely happens in a vacuum. Identifying the people who can help you reach a goal is an important component of achieving that goal. After putting off my dreamed-of goal of writing this book for more than five years, I finally decided that other people would have to be involved for it to be successful. I enlisted the support of my family and friends as well as that of people who agreed to read and comment on every chapter as it was written.

Liaisons with teachers, coaches, business associates, family, friends, and doctors, lawyers, or Indian Chiefs can be a deciding factor in achieving success at your endeavor. Losing weight without the dietary support of your family is difficult. Building a new home without a banker watching your checkbook with you is difficult. Learning to play the piano without a compassionate teacher is nearly impossible.

Working together increases both your satisfaction and your effectiveness in accomplishing your mission. As a precocious pre-teen, I spent many hours with my friends walking the uncharted territory of the railroad tracks in North Charleston, South Carolina. My mother discovered this fact only after I graduated from college, and she still had a compelling urge to smack the living daylights out of me. Russell Smith and I often made a game of seeing who could walk the furthest on a track without falling off.

We would walk heel-to-toe with our arms outstretched for balance. This simple childhood competition afforded us hours of pleasure and unspeakable bravery as we challenged each other and the Pennsylvania Railroad locomotives, which would bear down on us at a blazing five miles per hour near the railroad yard. The longest either of us ever walked down a single track was about thirty feet.

Little did we realize that the secret to walking the tracks for as far as we could see was just at our fingertips. If instead of competing, had we chosen to work together in liaison with one another, we could have joined hands across the tracks. Working as a two-kid symphony instead of one-kid soloists, our only restriction to traversing the train tracks limitlessly would have been patience and strength. We could have walked for miles if we had only realized the power of working together to achieve our goal.

Information

Los Angeles Times, January 2, 1998

Goal-setting Goal Eluding 'Reinvented' U.S. Agencies

"The Environmental Protection Agency plans to measure its success in protecting wetlands on the basis of how many acres of land it can set aside as federal sanctuaries each year — with virtually no thought about how many of these parcels may actually be at risk."

Most of us think we're fairly bright people. And most of us are. But none of us knows everything we need to know to accomplish everything we want to achieve. Giving yourself a "heads-up" about the information and knowledge necessary to reach a goal can forestall early failure.

When remodeling our home office, we decided to replace our fax machine with software that we operate right from the computer, which is connected to a data line all the time. Everyone agreed that this decision was a good move to make because it eliminated an extra piece of equipment that took up space and wasn't very pretty anyway. My first stop on this "fax software journey" was the Internet. After researching numerous software packages, I quickly realized that our options were numerous and a plethora of features and benefits was available.

This information gathering exercise led us to purchase a simple yet effective software package written specifically for our modem. By recognizing our need to gather information before plunging into action, we alleviated a problem experienced by many people who make the same kind of computer decisions. We discovered that many software packages couldn't reset the modem without custom commands written by people who speak and think in binary. This inability makes receiving more than one fax between re-boots difficult, and makes using your modem to access an online service impossible without shutting down the software first. Information was the king of our office when it came to fax software.

Watching a video on the basics of playing baseball, walking through the local parade of homes, visiting a college campus, learning about the stock market, and reading the classified ads are all examples of how you might gather information about your goal before you actually start to do it.

Many of us confuse activity with accomplishment. Action anxiety is a surefire way to derail a goal early in the process. Jean-Henry Fabre, a French naturalist, performed an experiment with processional caterpillars. These creatures follow one another head-to-tail as they journey from one place to another. He arranged these caterpillars in a circle, and in keeping with their name, they proceeded to walk around and around following each other to nowhere. When Fabre placed pine needles, the natural food of the bugs, in the middle of the circle they circum-navigated, they ignored it and continued to follow one another to their eventual death.

With the means to survive just inches away, they chose incessant activity over accomplishment. I see this choice made in business all the time. People go from idea generation to action in a matter of moments without serious forethought about what they're trying to achieve in the first place. I can't tell you the number of times I've started a project and ended up making seventeen dozen trips to the hardware store to finish it. (I defy anyone to install an underground sprinkler system without doing just that).

This information-gathering process is really a derivative of planning. For those people who have a natural pre-disposition to a Judging preference as identified on the Myers-Briggs Type Indicator, this activity comes naturally. For those who prefer Perception, it is a learned skill. We see this in our daily lives everywhere we look.

Most people spend significantly more time planning a wedding than they do a marriage. We invest countless hours gathering information about our upcoming vacation yet ignore information gathering about our continued relationships with one another. The average Super Bowl team invests three thousand hours every season planning for that four-hour event. They gather information, watch videos, and learn the strengths and weaknesses of each other and their opponents in their serious process to reach their goal.

Information about upcoming weddings, vacations, and Super Bowls are important, but they don't hold a candle to our discovery of what we can learn to enhance the effectiveness of marriages, family relationships, and life.

Don't confuse activity with accomplishment. What is at stake may be more than merely an event.

Deadline

Los Angeles Times, January 2, 1998
Goal-setting Goal Eluding 'Reinvented' U.S. Agencies
"The initial drafts were due last September 30th."

A goal without a deadline is a dream. Of the eight components of goal setting, the single most critical part that causes activity to happen is the deadline. Herb Cohen, author of *You Can Negotiate Anything*, enumerates three components of a negotiation—*Time, Information, and Power*.

With respect to time, he writes that most activity happens at, near, or even beyond a deadline. It is important to note that deadlines for goals must be set at smaller milestones (the yard-line part of SOLIDIFY). For example, a person with a goal of losing twenty-five pounds in twelve weeks, will often not bother to get started until eight or nine weeks into the process. In writing this book, my goal was to write five pages every day for a month. After a week of diligent early morning sessions, I found it easier and easier to begin writing later and later in the day. By the end of the third week, weekends had been sacrificed. By the fourth week, writing and editing five pages became a two-day rather than a one-day process. I found that even though I had deadlines to meet, it was a real temptation to put off my work until the deadline approached.

I have attended scores of committee or community service meetings only to discover that people with projects or reports to complete had begun their work only hours before the meeting convened. We see this in children as they finish their homework while riding the bus to school, in parents finishing their last-minute shopping before Christmas, in spouses as they make a mad dash through the kitchen and bedroom gathering things they've known all along needed to be gathered, and on the job as we observe our co-workers frantically putting the finishing touches on projects and reports only moments before they are due.

A friend and I developed an experiential team-training activity, which took about a year of our time and thousands of dollars to create. We finally found a company to run a pilot program with their managers. This organization, located in the midlands of North Carolina, was three hours from my friend's home and six hours from mine. I drove to Greg's home the day before we were to present a pilot, fully expecting everything to be ready to go as we put the finishing touches on our presentation.

Understanding his personal preference to be Perception rather than Judging, I should have anticipated the last-minute crunch to prepare our presentation. At eleven o'clock that night, we were designing and printing instructions at his dining room table in preparation for our five a.m. trip to Kinko's. On the three-hour trek to the client's office, I did the driving while he labored in the back seat assembling the workbooks.

We arrived in time to spend a grand total of ten minutes setting up our activity. The pilot was great, but my nerves were frazzled. We got the contract, and my friend, Greg, was in a celebratory mood all the way home.

Fortunately, deadlines cause activity to happen toward reaching a goal. Unfortunately, quality, productivity, or sanity is often sacrificed when activity is delayed until the last-minute. Last-minute activity is not always bad though. Some people, especially Perceptors, procrastinate until the pressure is on. These people almost always land on their feet and feel overwhelmingly energized from their successes.

The correlation between Judging and Perception with the

deadline portion of goal setting is important. Especially with children. As a child, my wife, Kathy, a strong Judger, spent weeks preparing term papers and science projects. If she had been forced to wait until the last few days before the deadline to begin her work, she would have produced a substandard assignment. It would have been frustrating to her and would have endangered her status as Valedictorian of her senior class. Megan, our older daughter, produces her best work at or near the deadline. Our efforts to coerce her into early work on assignments due weeks later produced the same results. Frustration and poor quality reports were the norm under those conditions. Her most stellar work came when she burned the midnight oil with the deadline quickly approaching.

This difference in Perceptors regarding expediency with respect to deadlines in no way demands that people with a Judging preference expend effort early or that Perceptors should wait until the last minute. It does, however, provide insight into when someone's best work might be accomplished. For either personality preference you can count on one fact, though. If a goal has been set and a deadline is not established at milestones along the way, very little activity will happen. A goal without a deadline is relegated to dream status.

Intrinsic

Los Angeles Times, January 2, 1998

Goal-setting Goal Eluding 'Reinvented' U.S. Agencies

"If all this makes you want to roll your eyes saying, 'Yep it sure sounds like the same old federal government we know,' then guess again. This time, it's the 'reinventing government' that is being put into place by President Clinton and the Republican-led Congress."

Susan Fowler, co-author of *Situational Self-Leadership®*, and I have had a running debate for years about this component of goal setting. For decades, the SMART acronym has been the mainstay of teaching people about goals. The first letter always represents Specific. Measurable or Motivating, Attainable or Achievable, Relevant, Realistic, or Resources, and Time-Bound or Trackable are represented by the other letters. Our disagreement was deeply rooted in the letter "M."

My perspective was that Measurable goals gave people milestones to track their progress, making the goal much easier to achieve in small portions rather than in one huge bite. Her perspective was that a goal must be Motivating and compelling for it to be truly worthwhile. We've gone around and around in our professional discussions on this subject and have probably expended much more energy than either of us could afford.

Susan wins. She bought a book for me entitled *Why We Do What We Do* by Edward L. Deci. His fourth chapter on the difference between intrinsic and extrinsic motivation makes sense. Intrinsic motivation toward reaching a goal comes from within. Simply stated, (actually, greatly over-simplified) the goal is something you really want to do.

Extrinsic motivation comes from somewhere else. An extrinsically motivated goal is not something you want to achieve, but something someone else thinks is important for you to accomplish. Paraphrasing his text, this example is the story of intrinsic motivation:

Two groups of children were asked to read passages from grade-school-level textbooks. One group was told that they would be tested and graded on their recollection of facts about the passage. The other group was simply asked to read it for fun. Those who learned the material without the expectation of having to recall it on a test displayed superior conceptual knowledge about the passage. Those who read the passage so that they might regurgitate the facts on a test scored far better on the rote memorization aspects of the quiz. This research tends to support the concept of *extrinsic* motivation in learning. Read on.

These children were revisited a week later. When tested about the passage they had read earlier, *every single one* of the children recalled less than on the original test.

Deci writes, "Stunningly, however, those who had learned expecting to be tested had forgotten much more. Their superior rote memorization was no longer in evidence a few days later. Evidently, they memorized the material for the test, and when the test was over they pulled the plug and let it drain out."

When motivated extrinsically to do something, these kids did a brain dump as soon as the test was over. Ensuring your goals are intrinsically rather than extrinsically motivated can give you the extra steam you need when you run up against roadblocks, especially if those obstacles are not foreseen.

This is not to say that all goals must be completely intrinsic. I can remember my mother making me practice the piano thirty minutes every day regardless of my desire to play baseball or ride my bike with friends. The goal of playing the piano was extrinsically motivated for me. Because of her continued support and encouragement coupled with my accomplishments and childhood skills, the goal slowly transformed from being extrinsically to intrinsically motivating.

Although it was hard to see then, I have twenty/twenty hindsight about that goal today. The hundreds of hours I could have spent playing outside were far better invested in music. Of course, I still got to play outside, but I had to reprioritize my day to allow for the piano first. As a child, I held a serious grudge against Mom for making me practice. As an adult, I owe her a debt of gratitude that can only be repaid when I or my children play for her.

Motivation to reach a goal is not limited to an individual experience. It can also be present in groups. Ask any coach of any sport, and he or she will tell you that members of a winning team draw from within for their most important plays. All of the pep talks in the world cannot motivate a team which isn't playing for the intrinsic value of winning. Extrinsic motivation on adult teams such as status, money, retirement, endorsements, and fan approval all play a role in superstars' performances. But in their soul, the reason they play the game and do it so well has very little to do with those things. Ask Michael Jordan what he was thinking about with three seconds left in the game as his final drive to the basket was being set up. Talk to Roger Banister about why he broke the four-minute mile. Inquire of Pele about his decision to coach children at the game of soccer. With all of these sports heroes, you will find their most compelling reasons to play and excel at their chosen career comes from within.

I serve on a committee of our church that is responsible for the staffing function. Our children's choir director recently resigned to move on to new ministries. She had taken a small group of a half-dozen preschool voices and, over the course of five years, created a world-class sixty-voice children's choir which performed not only in our church but also at community events. Some of the children were even admitted to the State Honors Chorus.

Upon her departure, our committee hired a new youth choir director with impeccable credentials. She is a delightful person who has worked with many children's choirs and is an accomplished musician. Two months into her tenure, she decided that things weren't working out as planned and made the decision to leave. Her departure, however, is not the focus of this story. What happened afterwards is.

Faced with a declining children's choir and increasing frustration from parents, we had to search deep inside to find out what we were really trying to accomplish here. Our original deliberations were centered on the need to continue the program because of its success in the past, as well as fulfilling the expectations of the children and their families in our congregation and the community. In other words, we were extrinsically motivated to achieve our goal of hiring the perfect person for the job because of everyone else's expectations.

After much soul searching and deliberation, we concluded that the most important reason to continue the program had very little to do with past performance. The most important motivation for our staffing disposition was the continued development of the children and their access to a youth group as they entered their teenage years. Our motivation really had very little to do with professional qualifications, performances, schedules, music selection, or practice facilities. Our heart-of-hearts told us that spiritual development and needs of children and families were the real reason for this program, and a choir director who shared this vision was a prerequisite to making it happen.

Today, two of our church members share responsibility for this program. As a committee, we are delighted. They are not in this for the money, and we are not in this for the control. We have an intrinsic plan on which to operate when it comes to our children. Our motivation, and the commitment of the new directors, emanates from within. It is intrinsic.

We both win, Susan. Thank you.

Feasible

Los Angeles Times, January 2, 1998

Goal-setting Goal Eluding 'Reinvented' U.S. Agencies

"The Defense Department continues to spend billions of dollars on new computers, but many of its most important functions, such as inventory control, are still accomplished largely by hand or with relatively primitive technology."

I've had some pretty outrageous goals for myself over the years. My first venture into a career outside of corporate America was a part-time project to create a video-training program that taught people how to interview for a job. My visions of grandeur were nothing short of an Emmy. Another hair-brained idea manifested itself in the form of buying land and developing a subdivision. Yet another was making tons of money investing in penny stocks.

None of these goals was impossible, but none of them was feasible for me to accomplish. All of them failed miserably. A worthwhile goal doesn't necessarily have to be visible from the point at which you start, but it darn sure should be within the realm of possibility. Pie-in-the-sky goals that have been reached by incredibly successful people are often touted as the path to a bright future. Indeed, for some, they are. For most, however, they are mere fallacies.

I'm approached at least once a week by people who have the latest and greatest idea to make millions of dollars and retire to a life of luxury by simply getting my friends and family involved in a business. Of course, when I run the numbers, I also need to enlist the population of three small states to make that level of success transpire. I've counseled many young entrepreneurs as they dreamed about chucking their jobs and seeking fortunes in the restaurant or consulting business. Although their enthusiasm is infectious, I find their heads firmly stuck in the clouds with their feet dangling below them still miles above the ground.

I write this chapter not to discourage anyone from reaching for the sky. Even the most outrageous goals can be met and surpassed with the right conditions and a healthy dose of luck. Mike Reich, a retired senior executive for an engineering division of the Navy, calls luck the point at which proper planning and opportunity meet one another. Proper planning while setting goals includes at least a minimal gut check to ensure it is worthy of consideration and feasibility.

For those of us who continually have ideas that could make

us either a millionaire or a pauper, I encourage the use of Pareto's curve. That's the 80/20 rule. Eighty percent of our accomplishments come from twenty percent of our effort. Eighty percent of our time is spent on activities that yield twenty percent of our results. Eighty percent of our enjoyment comes from 20 percent of our activities.

Try making 80 percent of your goals feasible, and let the 20 percent that are pipe dreams hang out around the fringes. Lou Holtz, one of the most successful college football coaches in history, tells the story about his tenure with the Arkansas Razorbacks. Upon arrival at the University of Arkansas, a place from which he holds many fond memories, he tells of his perception that although he had not landed squarely in the middle of hell, he could sure see it clearly from where he stood.

That's a great idea when setting feasible goals. Although you don't have to be standing squarely in the middle of feasibility, you sure should be able to see it from where you begin.

Yardlines

Los Angeles Times, January 2, 1998

Goal-setting Goal Eluding 'Reinvented' U.S. Agencies

"Under the legislation, agencies were to have submitted detailed reports setting out long-range goals and objectives and proposing ways for taxpayers to evaluate whether the bureaucrats they pay are meeting them. While compliance is improving, we have a long way to go to reach the point where every agency knows exactly what it is trying to accomplish and has a plan to reach measurable goals."

I don't profess to be a great football fan, but I do spend an occasional Saturday afternoon or Monday night enjoying a game. A common characteristic of every football field, regardless of where it resides, is a collection of hash marks known as yardlines.

Every team has the goal of crossing the goal line; the name

is no accident. To get there, they focus intense attention on ten-yard increments. Reaching these incremental goals allows them to continue their efforts towards achieving the big goal, a touch-down. They get four chances to accomplish these incremental goals.

Successful teams do not focus on trying to make a first down every time they snap the ball. They understand they have three golden opportunities to cross that ten-yard mini-goal, and they focus their early efforts on advancing the ball three to five yards at a time. By the time third down arrives, their strategy becomes a bit bolder, and upon their last chance at fourth down, the decision to run, pass, punt, or attempt a field goal is strate-gic.

This part of goal setting dovetails nicely with the intrinsic nature of a goal. Many people set lofty goals for themselves and mistakenly identify their points of accomplishment only at the end. Although the end is important, the minor achievements along the way can keep you focused and energized. Just like a football team celebrates mini-successes every time they achieve a first down. (Where else on the planet can we observe huge men slapping each other on the butt and flipping somersaults in the end-zone on national television?)

Without yardlines, a goal may be so huge that it becomes daunting. Deciding to lose twenty-five pounds can make the best of us reach for a second helping of chocolate pie without realiz-ing that it is really a series of mini-goals to lose two pounds per week. Five ounces a day is the yardline we are trying to reach.

Anonymous programs which help people overcome the negative aspects of everything from alcohol and drugs to smok-ing and over-eating share the same motto—"One day at a time." The goal of giving up a behavior that has been a part of your life for so long is overwhelming unless it is broken into smaller, manageable, and more realistic portions.

Teaching an eight-year old child to become an "all-star" begins with underhanded tosses and incremental goals to master grounders, fly balls, bunting, base running, and sliding. These are baseball's yardlines to a child. Making the honor roll consists of tomorrow's homework, Thursday's quiz, and next week's report. These are education's yardlines.

A successful relationship, whether personal or professional, begins with communication, understanding, shared values, listening, and *intentional* behaviors that support it. These are the milestones we share with each other at work and at home. I've seen so many families who have forgotten how to do this.

The question "How was your day?" inquires most often about the attainment of yardlines. Nagging one another about money without recognition of the milestones reached toward your financial goals creates frustration and resentment. Withholding praise until a child brings home a report card makes it difficult for her to see the benefit of working hard to make a ninety-five on next week's paper. Even cutting the grass is easier when you see it in terms of the front and back yard rather than an afternoon in the hot sun. Yardlines are important.

On the surface, it looks like this division is an awful lot of effort just to work on a goal. I'm encouraging you to enjoy the benefits of doing just that. Notice, please, that I did not say you should pay the price of doing that.

To work diligently on your goals at work and with your family, an attitude of *benefit* should be adopted. For decades, I've heard that one must pay the price for good health—no pain, no gain. It's also been said that you pay the price for a good relationship. It is written somewhere that you pay the price for success.

That's hogwash.

We pay the price for poor health. We enjoy the *benefits* of good health. We pay the price for destroyed relationships. We enjoy the *benefits* of healthy friendships and marriages. We pay the price for failure. We enjoy the *benefits* of success.

SOLIDIFY… Specific, Obstacles, Liaisons, Information, Deadlines, Intrinsic, Feasible, Yardlines… Magnetize them to your refrigerator. Commit them to memory.

These are things that can help you and your family enjoy: the *benefits* of reaching your goals, and perhaps, keep you from paying the price of not realizing them. Take this lesson home to them, and enjoy the benefits of doing so.

CHAPTER ELEVEN

Friday, 11:02 p.m.

The telephone rings.

Rachel, age fifteen, is calling home, and her father, David, answers.

"Daddy, Daddy, he's hitting me," she says breathlessly. "Please make him stop. We've been driving for hours," she sobs hysterically. "I don't know where we are. Please help me, Daddy," she screams. "Make him stop, Daddy!"

Click.

One minute later, at 11:03 p.m., David calls 911. He speaks rapidly to the city police dispatcher on the line.

"This is David Johnson, 1427 Towne Circle. I just received a panic cell phone call from my daughter. She is in a car with someone who has been hitting her. They've been driving for hours," he says in a strained voice." Please send someone who can help. Hurry! We don't know where she is."

Friday, 11:06 p.m.

David is speaking with his wife Diane, age 38, Rachel's mother.

"Rachel has been kidnapped. Someone's hurting her right now," He says in a low voice, struggling to find words. "She's in a car with John and God knows who else. The police officers are on the way. See if you can find her tenth grade pictures from last week and call John's parents."

Sunday, 11:32 p.m.

The telephone rings. David, who hasn't slept in 63 hours, answers the call on the first ring.

It is Birmingham Police Captain Gerald Cable calling.

"Mr. Johnson, we've found Rachel, and she's safe and relatively OK. Her 'supposed' boyfriend kidnapper dumped her in the parking lot at a mall in Birmingham. The hospital says she's in good condition. She's hungry, bruised, dehydrated and pretty scared. They'll release her as soon as you provide instructions on how to get her home."

Captain Cable's voice lowers to almost a whisper. "Mr. Johnson," he says almost apologetically, "she had traces of some pretty serious drugs in her system. She's sober now, and although you didn't ask me for advice, if she were my daughter, I'd get her in a rehab center as soon as she gets home."

Sunday, 11:38 p.m.

David needs to get Rachel home right away and calls US Airways.

"Good evening," he says to the airline representative. "This is David Johnson. My number is 610-476-7775."

He pauses, waiting impatiently for the computer to catch up to his racing mind and hears the agent confirm his address and phone number.

"I'd like to make arrangements for my daughter, Rachel, to catch an eight a.m. flight home from Birmingham tomorrow morning," he says. "Yes, charge that to my American Express on file. Law enforcement officials will escort her to the gate in Birmingham. I'll meet her at the gate here when her flight arrives. Thank you."

Sunday, 11:54 p.m.

Back porch of their home at 1427 Towne Circle, David and Diane holding hands, silent, abundant tears falling softly to the floor, his and hers mixing at their feet, hearts clenched so tightly they could hardly breathe, staring into each other's eyes but not seeing each other . . . they only see Rachel in their mind's eye.

"What did we do wrong?" they begged of each other over and over again. "What did we do that was so wrong?"

✱✱✱

Step Number Four

Since the 1960s, workers and managers have been learning the value of effective feedback and communication and the importance of a positive work environment. It seems that some companies have gone overboard and become almost apologetic for providing structure and firm instruction, choosing praise and inclusion in everything they do, no matter how mediocre the performance or skill.

Others migrate to the opposite end of the spectrum, maintaining their autocratic, stagnant, and somewhat threatening cultures. Praise and positive feedback are *not* bad things. They require skills that must be mastered to be used effectively and must be meaningful to be believed. Hollow praise falls on deaf ears. Praise for mediocre performance encourages even more mediocrity.

A core supportive skill of providing effective feedback, especially to beginners, is the ability to praise performance that is either right or approximately right while redirecting incorrect or inappropriate behavior. The ability to provide meaningful praise is fairly straightforward.

First, tell people specifically what they did right.

Second, explain the importance of that behavior and the impact it had on you, the organization, or others around them.

Third, express your appreciation.

Fourth, ask them to explain how or why they did what they did.

Finally, express confidence in future performance and behavior *without* adding more to their plate, and especially *without* following it up with a reprimand.

Effective leaders have practiced this simple process all over the world. As with most leadership skills, it's not rocket science. It is, however, awkward and uncomfortable until you've mastered the process. While these five simple steps are all important, one stands out as critical.

David and Diane related the story of Rachel's recovery. She was placed in an in-patient treatment facility where family and group therapy was part of the counseling regimen. In one group session, Rachel looked at her father and told him this: ""Dad, you never taught me how to feel good about myself."

David's defensive and angry response was predictable:

> What do you mean? Every time you made an A on a paper, didn't we plaster it all over the refrigerator with magnets explaining how proud we were of you? Every time you practiced a song and played it all the way through, weren't we in the living room clapping our hands showing how pleased we were? Every time you hit a home run, caught a ball, or made a basket, weren't we in the stands cheering you on, buying pizza, and telling you how proud we were?

Rachel responded, "Yeah, Dad, you were so proud. What about me?"

David tells me that was one of life's defining moments. How many times had he sat in a classroom listening to some instructor teaching the value of providing positive feedback while building the self-esteem of his people? How many times had he followed the five step process, including Step Number Four, making sure that his employees understood the value of what they'd done? How many times had he come home elated, telling Diane about some direct-report whose day he had made simply by recognizing and discussing her good performance?

The answer—hundreds of times.

In Rachel's first fifteen years of life, how many times could he remember asking her how it felt to make an A? Why she practiced so hard to play a song? What was it like to get a hit, catch a ball, or make a basket? How many times had he done at home what he knew so well to do at work to build the self-esteem of the most important people in his world? How many times had he done Step Number Four with his family?

The answer—never.

He began to understand that Rachel had spent the first twelve years of her life trying to make her parents feel good about her performance. At about age twelve, coping with hormones, peers, an unruly body, and zits, Rachel's biological clock forced her to stop depending on her parents and start depending on her most important source of feedback—teenage peers.

Having spent the past three years talking to adolescent teenagers, David realized that he had not prepared Rachel to feel good about herself without his or Diane's intervention. In turn, young teenagers are rarely as supportive as David and Diane had been to their daughter. Not having the ability to feel good about herself, having never really been taught by her parents to do so, and having a peer group that did not see the importance of praise and positive feedback, Rachel turned to an external source to feel good. Drugs.

John, the boyfriend and kidnapper (now in prison) assumed a critical third role in Rachel's life. He was also her supplier of good feelings.

Rachel's younger sister, Marcia, has absolutely no doubt about the destructive nature of drugs. She also understands the need for self-esteem. Her life has been irrevocably affected by Rachel's crisis. But the effect has been positive. She has learned to do Step Number Four for herself. David and Diane taught her how by using the process daily to "catch her doing something right" (one of Ken Blanchard's favorite phrases) and tell her about it.

As in business, we learn our most valuable lessons from our mistakes. David and Diane don't take responsibility for Rachel's drug use, kidnapping, or teenage rebellion. They do, however, recognize the role they played and the deficiency in self-esteem they helped to create. Part of their recovery involves the way they provide parenting leadership to Marcia.

The silver lining on this cloud took a year to be found. David and his family now see their experience as a blessing. Rachel picked up her ten-year chip from Alcoholics Anonymous recently. Once again, David and Rachel wept together. The price Rachel paid—lost innocence, violence, and psychological crisis—is far less than the price many people pay as adults. The grown-up price for Rachel's behavior is often paid in prison, with a lost career, through destructive relationships, with abandoned children, and by financial ruin.

Providing positive feedback isn't complete until you've taken the time to do Step Number Four. *Find* the time to do this for the people with whom you work.

Make the time to do it with your children.

CHAPTER TWELVE

"Hi, Honey. How was your day?"

"*Just Fine!*"

"Great, my day was just fine, too. We had an awesome announcement at work. Everyone is going to get a week off with pay after Christmas. Isn't that great?"

"Sure. I'm just tickled to death."

"I thought you would be. We can take some time to visit your parents and maybe spend a few days skiing with the kids. It'll be a great holiday."

"I'm sure we'll have fun."

"You bet we will. Why don't you talk to your mom tonight and see if we can spend a few extra days with them before we head to the mountains."

"Okay."

"What went on during your day?"

"Nothing much."

"Well, mine was wall-to-wall activity. I'm glad I got there fifteen minutes early to go through my e-mail before everyone else got in. We had three unannounced meetings today, and two customers stopped by and wanted at tour of the plant."

"That's nice."

"Is something wrong, sweetheart?"

"What would give you that idea?"

"You just seem kind of quiet tonight."

"Well, there's nothing you can do about it NOW anyway. The damage has already been done."

"Okay, if you say so. What's for supper?"

"I'll tell you what's for supper! Bologna sandwiches and potato chips. You know today is the day you're supposed to stop by the grocery store on the way home to pick up something for dinner. You've been so self-absorbed that you just forgot about the rest of us. When are you going to stop thinking only of yourself and start being a little more considerate of your family? I've worked hard all day too, you know, and the kids had a really bad day at school. Then you walk in empty-handed with a soliloquy about your conquest of the day, acting like we've got nothing better to do than listen to you."

"Whoa! What did I do?"

"Aren't you listening? I thought we agreed that you'd stop by the store and pick up some chicken and vegetables for stir fry tonight. Do you think dinner just magically appears when you walk in the door? This was your responsibility, and you blew it."

"Wait a minute. I've had a busy day, and it's not fair to walk in the house with you armed to the teeth and loaded for bear about dinner. Can't we just have leftovers tonight?"

"That's not the issue. What we're talking about here is you taking responsibility for your commitments. You said you would handle supper tonight, and you let us all down again. This isn't about groceries. It's about you!"

"Okay, I get it. Let's just make a tuna casserole. We've got all the stuff we need in the pantry and refrigerator. No problem, is it? See, I had it figured out all along, didn't I?"

"No! You are absolutely clueless about figuring anything out. You haven't heard a word I've said."

"Sure I have, Honey. Why don't you put your feet up for a few minutes, and I'll fix supper. I don't mind at all. You've had a busy day too, I'm sure."

"Is anyone listening in this house? I feel like I'm talking to a wall."

"Of course I'm listening, Honey. Should I fix a salad, too?"

✳✳✳

Is Anybody Out There?

We've all been either the perpetrator or the victim in conversations like this. It seems that when one person is talking, the other person is simply waiting for his turn to speak. The foundation of effective communication begins with listening. Listening is one of the most supportive behaviors you can adopt and is an important skill to practice with someone who has a lack of motivation or confidence. It is a wonderful way to stand beside people when they need your support the most.

Volumes have been written on the subject. You can study senders, receivers, filters, paradigms, reflection, spontaneity, refraction, words, inflection, semantics, or dozens of other components that can be assessed and measured in verbal communication. Rather than addressing each of them, I suggest you begin improving your communication skills by first learning to listen for understanding and then learning to speak so that you are understood. This is one of the habits from Steven Covey's *Seven Habits of Highly Effective People.*

No leadership seminar would be complete without the obligatory module on communication. With such a broad subject, most of these workshop segments are woefully fragmented or incredibly simplistic. Flavor-of-the-month is a term often used to describe seminars with the newest, latest, and greatest twist on it. This chapter will deal with four tried and true listening and speaking skills necessary to be an effective communicator.

First, understand that listening is an art form. Every union negotiator who ever sat across the table from management understands the importance of listening. This statement is true because the message being sent is often different from the message being heard. Acknowledge listening is a simple technique used to convey understanding; in acknowledge listening a person responds with a sentence beginning with a phrase that helps him to reiterate or clarify what he has heard, rather than presenting his own opinions. It takes minutes to learn but a lifetime to master.

As children, we learned the importance of, and rules for, polite conversation. Anyone who has participated in a dinner conversation with a two-year-old understands these rules. Children at this age are trying on new words and combining these words into sentence fragments as they relay their thoughts to others. This practice is a totally new concept for small children and is one that fascinates them beyond belief. A two-year old talks incessantly about anything that pops into her little mind, and she fully expects the world around her to be enraptured by her musings. When the entire family is being held captive at the dinner table, a two-year-old can really shine.

Most parents manage this verbal avalanche with new rules for dining together. Mom, dad, brother, or sister will interrupt the chattering toddler to explain the newly created edict.

"It's not your turn to talk. We are all going to take a turn, and when we've finished with what we want to say, then you can have a turn."

This simple, yet effective, rule of conversation will ensure that everyone gets an opportunity to speak. It also ensures that while one person is talking, other family members, instead of listening, are formulating their own thoughts into words so that they might speak when it comes their turn. This fact is especially true for the two-year old.

Therefore, we are taught at an early age that it is not necessarily important that we listen to what is being said. It is critical, though, that we adhere to the rules of polite conversation by waiting for our turn to speak. Unfortunately, most of us carry this rule forward into our adult lives and even perpetuate the insanity by teaching *our* children the same rule.

Acknowledge listening is a tool that alleviates this phenomenon.

Instead of formulating your own opinions and responses while someone else is talking, you should make eye contact, lean slightly toward the speaker, nod understandingly, and respond with a statement structured with one of the following phrases: "sounds like," "that must be," "in other words," "so you think," "then you feel," or "then it is."

If this technique had been used in the conversation at the beginning of the chapter, an early response might have sounded like one of these statements:

- "Sounds like something is on your mind."
- "That must be frustrating for you when I do that."
- "In other words, I screwed up big-time tonight, didn't I?"
- "So you think I should've acted more responsibly."
- "You feel pretty angry about dinner, don't you?"
- "Then it's my responsibility to make up for forgetting about dinner tonight."

These responses won't completely defuse the conflict, but they sure might make the rest of the evening a little more hospitable. What happens when you acknowledge someone else's spoken thoughts is you validate that he's been heard. Anyone who has ever had the displeasure of arguing with a teenager understands this.

Raging hormones, changing bodies, unsavory peer groups, and general discontent plague most teenagers at some point in that hormone-ridden portion of their lives. When in an argument with a parent over some issue (generally about being treated fairly and as an adult rather than a child), they will present the same argument fourteen different ways without stating a single new idea. But all the burden of an ineffective conversation shouldn't be placed on the shoulders of the teen. Parents are just as guilty, but this inadequacy seems to be a function of the gene pool inherited by us all from as far back as the days of the cave man. Most parents will recognize the following conversation:

Request, *"Can I go to the mall with Esmeralda tonight?"*

One word response: *"No."*

One word question: *"Why?"*

One word answer: *"Because."*

Two word question: *"Because why?"*

Four word response: *"Because I said so!"*

This discourse almost always leads to some form of an argument that generates anger, stress, and feelings of unfairness about being treated that way by the other person. The teenager thinks the parent is being unreasonable, and the parent thinks that the teenager doesn't recognize the risk or appreciate the responsibilities necessary to undertake such an activity on his own. In other words, no one is listening, and all are waiting for *their* turn to talk.

By injecting an acknowledge phrase after each main point, the adult-in-training contributes to the conversation. By doing so, he can sideline the emotions of being treated unfairly and focus instead on the issues at hand. Will the teenager defer peacefully? Probably not. But at least the parent's blood pressure and pucker factor will remain at manageable levels for the evening. We also experience the inexcusably sadistic byproduct of frustrating the heck out of our teenagers by letting them know that they have been heard. We then force them to come up with new arguments rather than presenting the same old ones over and over with a slightly different twist to each reiteration.

Teaching this tactic to each other can be fun. Try a dinner time game of allowing people to respond only with an acknowledgment of what has been said earlier. The rule in this game is that no one can inject her ideas into the conversation until previous comments have been acknowledged by someone at the table. You can even prompt elementary age children with a small note card displaying acknowledge phrases written in crayon. This life skill goes a long way toward making family relationships more pleasant and reducing the frustration we all experience in the midst of conflict when we don't believe the other person understands or appreciates our point of view.

Skilled listening is important, but other things must be understood and mastered to make someone a good communicator. Getting your point across is far more involved than merely saying the words. Speaking to be understood is an art form.

According to Albert Morabean, a researcher on the subject, there are three components of verbal communication:
1. Words — your thoughts as verbally articulated
2. Emotion and tone — Inflection and volume of the words
3. Body language — the position and movement of your body

His research, which has been validated time and again over the past three decades, led to an understanding of the importance of each of these components in verbalizing thought. To believe the statistics, you must first buy into the premise of effective communication, which it is this: *"It is not important what you say when you verbally communicate, but it is very important what the listener understands you to have said."*

In other words, if you say something that is not understood the same way you intended it to be, the effectiveness of your words is negligible.

To measure the relationship between words, emotion and tone, and body language, an experiment is necessary. Three similar groups are needed. With each group, sit them down and deliver a brief speech on any subject, presenting it in differing manners. You might even read an article from a newspaper. I've done this in communication workshops using this text:

> The purpose of discipline is to obtain compliance with established rules of conduct. Your role is to promote proper conduct according to the expectations previously set by you and the organization. Your role is not to punish people. To accomplish this goal, it is important that a progressive disciplinary system be established. This system should be an escalating process that begins with relatively painless, yet effective, communication about infractions. Your response after each repeated infraction should escalate in seriousness and imposed consequences. For this reason, organizations issue a verbal reprimand for initial tardiness, but later impose suspensions and termination if said tardiness continues.

With the first group, I quote this paragraph while facing away from the group and speaking in the most monotonous and boring voice I can muster. When I am finished, I give them a test on what I have just said.

The second group gets exactly the same words, also spoken with my back to them. In this lecture, however, I add inflection and volume, punctuating each major point with variations and pauses. When I am finished, they get the same test.

The third and final group experiences this lecture while I face them. I move about the room using gestures, such as holding my hand up with one finger extended while saying the word *important* and making a chopping motion while saying the word *termination*. This group gets words, emotion and tone, and body language throughout the message. They also get the test.

Statistical analysis of the test scores from all three groups reveals the percentile relationship among the three components of verbal communication used when speaking:

1. Words — 7 percent
2. Emotion and tone — 38 percent
3. Body language — 55 percent

In other words, 93 percent of a person's understanding of what you say has nothing whatsoever to do with what you say, but everything to do with how you say it. The message you speak is best understood by hearing and observing your voice, posture, facial expressions, and gestures in addition to your words. We've all attended boring, mundane, "watching paint dry" training programs. Most of us have also participated in dynamic and interesting programs. I venture to say that the instructors in both the best and worst workshops you've ever attended had very different communication skills. The best probably had excellent mastery of voice and presence in the room. The worst probably stood behind a podium and droned on forever with little change in his voice or use of his hands. He may have even read his presentation.

Why is it, then, when someone has really important things to say before a group, she often spends countless hours composing the words and invests only a cursory glance on her presentation of those words? When given the opportunity to choose between the spoken and the non-verbal message as the truth, people will almost always choose the non-verbal message as gospel and relegate the actual spoken words to some form of prevarication.

As parents of small children, we understand this well. When a four-year-old is questioned about his artistic creation freshly applied to his bedroom wall, he will emphatically deny any involvement with his words while visibly cringing with his body. At this age, children haven't learned to make their bodies match their messages, and the body's message wins hands down when there's a discrepancy between the two.

The ramifications of body language and emotion and tone on verbal communication are serious at home as well as at work. It seems that when we have something very important to convey, we lower our voices and invoke a serious tone and posture. Even in a business setting in which people see each other every day, e-mail messages sometimes cripple communication. Writing instead of speaking a message face-to-face, discounts 93 percent of the potential for that message to be understood clearly. It is not to say that important information cannot be conveyed in writing, but it does suggest that our most impactful messages should be done in real life rather than on paper or electronically.

Acknowledge listening, words, emotion and tone, and body language are beneficial in all walks of life at any age. In families, these four tenets of communication are a prerequisite to reducing conflict, being understood, and understanding others. Continuous education is a whetstone for the mind, and developing your communication skills throughout all walks of your life creates a superb edge allowing for effective interaction along the journey.

CHAPTER THIRTEEN
April 8, 1978
Jerry's 4:45 p.m. telephone conversation to his father.

Jerry: "They accepted our offer! This is so exciting, Dad! Lisa and I have been living in apartments since we got married five years ago. It's been hard to save our money, but we finally got enough to make a 10 percent down payment on the house. We're getting a real deal. The whole thing is only going to cost us $33,500, and the house payment is only a few more dollars than our rent was."

Father: "How much is your payment, son?"

Jerry: "It's only $312 dollars a month, and that includes our taxes and insurance. I know it's expensive, but we're tired of living in apartments, and this is a great starter home."

Father: "You're right, Jerry. That's a lot of money. I think you're making a mistake."

Jerry: "You're kidding! This is a great opportunity to get into a house. I'm making $15,000 a year now. I think we can afford it."

Father: "I know you're excited, son, but have you thought about all the expenses that come with home ownership? You don't even own a lawnmower. You'll have to buy curtains, tools, and furniture. What are you going to do for a refrigerator?"

Jerry: "We'll manage, Dad. After all, you did the same thing when you were younger, didn't you?"

Father: "That's not the issue right now. I think you should
            wait until you can afford it before you make this
            huge decision. Why don't you keep looking until
            you can find a house with a payment about the same
            as mine?"

Jerry: "How much is your payment?"

Father: "It's $120 dollars a month."

Jerry: "That means you think we can afford a $15,000
            mortgage, doesn't it? Have you seen what a $15,000
            house looks like in 1978? Our apartment is nicer
            than any home like that, Dad."

Father: "Then you should just save your money until you
            can afford to make a down payment that will keep
            your mortgage payments around a hundred dollars.
            That's what I think you should do."

Jerry: "Dad, I love you. But you are way out of your league
            on this one. That might have worked well thirty
            years ago when you bought your first house, but
            today's world is a lot more expensive than that. If
            we wait to save the down payment or find a bargain
            like you're describing, Lisa and I will retire living in
            apartments."

Father: "I just hope you're not being irresponsible about
            this. You've never owned a home before, have you? I
            think you should heed my advice."

Jerry: "Thanks, Dad. We'll think about it."

    Later that evening. . .

Jerry: "Can you believe it, Sweetheart? We've been mar-
            ried five years, and Dad it is still trying to tell me
            how to do things. He's living in the dark ages."

    At the same time, a hundred miles away. . .

Father: "Can you believe it, Sweetheart? We've been married thirty years, and you'd think our son would have enough judgment to listen to sound device. He's got his head in the clouds on this one."

**

Letting Go and Grabbing Hold

Of all the leadership skills a person might master, delegation is the most terrifying and rewarding. We delegate to someone by giving away our responsibility, authority, and resources. One without the others is not delegation. Many managers attempt to delegate to their direct reports but allow them only limited authority to make any decision or expend resources without approval, giving away responsibility without authority. It's a method used to protect the manager from failure while holding an employee responsible. It also sets the manager up to receive credit if success is achieved. It's no wonder that giving away responsibility without granting appropriate levels of authority can cripple an organization's productivity and morale.

Abdication is often disguised as delegation. Assigning people tasks by simply outlining them and instructing them to get back with you if they have a question or problem is not delegation. The process is a little more involved than that.

Delegation is not only the manager's responsibility, but also the employee's. Letting go is worthless until someone is willing to grab hold.

In organizations where dictatorial managers have created anarchy, it may take a long time to get front-line people to accept delegation. Many employees have been taking the fall for their manager's ineptitude for generations. If this event has happened time and again to someone, it should come as no surprise that he confronts sincere delegation with a healthy dose of skepticism. In other words, his manager may be perfectly willing to let go of responsibility, authority, and resources, but the employee is not willing to accept it.

To make both sides of delegation work smoothly, a four step process should be adopted. It's a GAME plan, referring to Goal, Action, Monitor, and Empower.

Goal

The longest chapter in this book deals with goal-setting. When delegating, an agreed-upon goal is the prerequisite for both manager and employee. All eight SOLIDIFY goal setting bases should be touched when delegating—Specific, Obstacles, Liaisons, Information, Deadlines, Intrinsic, Feasible, and Yardlines.

Action

Nothing happens until someone does something. Too many people go into "analysis paralysis" when delegating. Details about activity toward achieving the task should be outlined and agreed upon.

Monitor

It is frustrating to all individuals concerned when the first feedback on the task comes upon completion. Monitoring stations should be set up along the way, often at the yardlines, for the employee to check in with the manager to report progress. This review allows managers and employees to cover their respective rear ends. It also allows them to adjust the course of action should problems occur.

Empower

This overused buzz-word of the 1980s is very important when delegating. Successfully letting go of responsibility, authority, and resources includes securing a clear agreement from both people of the expectations of credit, blame, decision-making authority, time, money, staff, and physical resources. Giving someone a task on which she will be held responsible without agreeing on these criteria usually creates failure or poor quality results.

These four steps can be accomplished by either party. Although they appear to be cumbersome, they can actually be completed in just a few minutes.

(Goal)"John, I'd like for you to check my e-mail while I'm on vacation in Africa next week. I've assigned you a temporary password so you can log in under my name, and you have respond rights on the system. Jim will help you out if you have any problems. I expect a few questions from Harry about your project, and I thought you'd want to respond while I'm gone. I use the same e-mail program you do, so it should be no problem. (Action) Just check it three times a day, and you'll be fine. You can log in from any terminal in the building or through the exchange server if you like. (Monitor) Leave me a voice message at the end of each day, and I'll check in from the satellite telephone. (Empower) It shouldn't take but a few minutes, and you have the authority to respond to anything that comes up unless it deals with personnel or budget issues. Thanks for handling this for me. Jennifer and I have been looking forward to this Safari for a year, and it's great that I've got someone like you who I can count on while we're gone."

This request is an example of a manager's taking responsibility for delegating all of the steps to a direct report. It takes only two minutes to delegate like this. Actually, the entire conversation could have been turned around to come from the employee and have been just as effective. Of course, delegating e-mail is much simpler than complex tasks or assignments. More complicated jobs require significantly more feedback and collaboration rather than simply delineated instructions.

What's this concept got to do with families?

A manager's goal with her people is to develop them from enthusiastic, yet ineffective beginners to proficient employees with positive attitudes, enabling them to operate successfully within the organization's culture. Parenting is no different.

The goal of a parent is to take an enthusiastic, yet inexperienced baby and develop that child into a proficient adult with a positive attitude and similar values to the family so he can operate successfully in our society. The major difference between parenting and employment is the time allowed to achieve this goal. In business, you are allowed a probationary period. In our families, most get eighteen to twenty-two years to accomplish this task.

We empower each other based on *when* the other person is ready to grab hold of the responsibility, authority, and resources we are ready to give up. A seventeen-year-old daughter may be figuratively escorted to the front door on Saturday morning with the following instruction:

"It's a beautiful day outside. I know you're planning to meet your friends at the mall and catch a movie this afternoon. Check and with us once in a while and be home in time for dinner."

If we've done our job as parents, a conversation like this would be perfectly appropriate. Our quest is to teach our children to behave responsibly and safely in society, and a seventeen-year old is quickly approaching the time when she will have to do this on her own. Previous conversations should have included the "rules" and all the other components of a GAME plan. When delegating to this daughter, a quick review of the deadline and monitoring process is all that is really necessary.

"It's a beautiful day outside. I know you're planning to meet your friends at the playground and watch cartoons this afternoon. Check in with us once in a while and be home in time for dinner."

Can you imagine holding this conversation with a five-year-old child? I hope not! The reason we delegate this task to a seventeen-year old and withhold responsibility, authority, and resources from the five-year-old is simple. The older child is ready to grab hold, and although the younger child thinks she is ready, she actually does not have the life skills necessary to stay safe on her own without supervision.

How many times have we delegated something to someone else without touching all the bases? The result was often a comment like "That's not what you told me to do." By establishing a GAME plan in delegating and reviewing that game plan when repeating a delegated task, confusion and frustration can be alleviated.

Just as we wouldn't delegate our responsibilities, authority, and resources to someone who is not ready to grab hold of them, we should also refrain from withholding those things when someone is ready to accept them. Back seat drivers, over-controlling parents, enthusiastic homework helpers, and micromanagers all tend to give too much direction while releasing too little responsibility, authority, and resources. When this trade-off happens, it drives people crazy.

My wife and I share the household duties. When cleaning up the kitchen, we approach it differently. I wash dishes first and wipe down counters last. She does it the other way around. It's almost comical to remember the times we've stumbled over each other when working together on the kitchen. We both learned early in our marriage, however, that if the end result were the same, we should each be allowed to approach it in our own way. If I have the delegated task of cleaning the kitchen one night, I get to define my own process to make it happen. If she has the job, she does it her way. When we do it together, we split the job down the middle and she does the wiping down while I do the washing. We are competent, motivated, and confident at this task, so neither of us should be meddling in the other's process. In other words, we delegate to each other.

Kathy is a superb driver, but she drives me bananas in traffic. I tend to be a more aggressive driver while she tends to drive much more defensively. Neither of us has ever had an accident, and we both learned long ago to suffer our differences in silence rather than instructing each other on how to drive. When it comes to driving, we delegate to the driver.

When we delegate, we are concerned with results. The process to get those results is of secondary concern *if the process supports the values and traditions of the family.* I've seen teenage sons take the family car to a friend's house to wash it so they wouldn't have to listen to Dad telling them how it should be done. I've seen husbands close the door so they could work on a project without their wives telling them how to do it. Some wives refuse to drive with their husbands in the car because it just causes too much stress. I've also seen children sneak behind their parents' backs to do something not because their parents would disapprove but because the children want to do it their way.

These situations were created by people's wanting to direct the activities of someone who felt the job should have been delegated. Someone was unwilling to let go to someone else who was ready to grab hold.

I've also seen husbands give up their lifelong dream of playing a guitar because they didn't sign up for lessons. I've heard of wives who abandoned their later-life college degrees because they were failing algebra and did not seek tutoring. I've observed children quit their baseball teams and drop out of piano classes because there was no one to practice with them.

These situations are created when someone needs direction and support and instead gets the responsibility, authority, and resources to work alone *before* they are ready for it.

Knowing when to delegate is the secret to doing it successfully. We should give away responsibility, authority, and resources when the persons to whom we are giving them have achieved competence, motivation, and confidence that they can perform the task on their own. If any one of these three criteria are not met, we set ourselves up for failure.

At some point in time, nearly all people are delegated the task of performing most of the life skills they need to live successfully in our society. Unfortunately, many people fail only because they've never had the opportunity to succeed on their own. Many widows have discovered this phenomenon when they are unexpectedly required to manage the finances of their family. More than half of all college students drop out before graduating, often because they were not prepared for academic or social life away from home. Thousands of teenagers turn to devastating lifestyles trying to grab hold of responsibility, authority, and resources before they are ready to accept them.

Perhaps the most difficult natural task parents will address is delegating life to their child as he or she gets older. Successful families recognize that this process of delegation starts when a child is a toddler. We delegate the tasks of tying shoes, going to the bathroom, dressing, eating, and eventually move into walking, driving, studying, managing money, developing spiritually, and forming and maintaining relationships.

As we delegate these most important things in life to our children, it is important that parents recognize their role to delegate responsibly. Of course, my role as a father is to teach my daughters the values and behaviors they need to live successfully in our society. It is also my job to teach them how a dad behaves. They learn from me how a husband should treat his wife and from Kathy how a wife should treat her husband. Although we will talk about these things from time to time, our daily demonstration of the values we hold dear is one of the most important things we can do as we eventually delegate the responsibility of choosing life's path to our children.

Although we would like to believe that we get to start fresh every time we delegate something new to someone, we are actually building upon everything we have formerly done in the relationship with this person. A manager delegating a task to a subordinate after having spent years blaming subordinates for failures will not be nearly as effective as another manager doing the same thing after having spent years accepting responsibility for the actions of his or her people. An over-controlling parent who finally delegates to an older child gets a completely different result than the parent who has been consistently delegating small tasks throughout the child's life.

Delegating the task of choosing someone with whom a child wants to spend the rest of her life is not an event. Delegating careers, spiritual beliefs, parenting styles, and responsible behaviors are not activities. Delegation is a *process* that begins at birth, is shaped throughout childhood and adolescence, and is solidified through the values and behaviors we demonstrate throughout life.

It should be done carefully and intentionally with your family. When they are ready, let go. Until then, teach them along the way to grab hold.

CHAPTER FOURTEEN

"I can't believe you did that! We just talked about this last week."

"I know we did, but I've had a thousand things on my mind and just forgot about it."

"That is no excuse. I went to a lot of trouble to set this thing up. My whole family is driving in on Thursday for the party. You had no right to schedule a trip the same day."

"I'll be home by 6:00, Jean. What's the big deal? They won't get here until then anyway!"

"Do you think things just happen by themselves around here? I'm taking the day off to clean up and decorate. You were supposed to stay home to help me."

"I can still help you. It'll just have to be the day before. Come on, Jean. They're my family too. They'll understand if everything isn't perfect."

"That's not the point. You told me you would help, and now you'll be gone the entire day. It's not fair for you to abandon me when we agreed that you'd be here."

"I know I agreed, but this trip is important too. It was scheduled for next week, but the client had to rearrange the meeting. This Thursday was the only time we can get together this month. What was I supposed to do? Tell him to take a hike?"

"I don't care what you tell your client. You obviously have your priorities in different places than I thought. This is Tammy's graduation party for just our family, for goodness sake. Don't you think you could put in a little effort to make it nice?"

"Now *you* are not being fair! Can't you understand why I need to be gone that day?"

"Talk about not being fair! Can't you understand why I need you here that day?"

"Well, obviously you think throwing a family party is more important than my work. You certainly don't have much appreciation for my efforts, do you?"

"The party is irrelevant here, Barry. When are you going to start thinking about your family when you schedule all of these trips? I'm talking about honoring your commitments to us."

"And I thought my commitment to you was to provide for our home and lifestyle! That's what I was doing when I scheduled the trip."

"No you weren't. You agreed to that trip without two seconds of thought about us."

"How do you know what I was thinking?"

"I don't! But I do know what you weren't thinking. You go ahead and take your little trip. We'll get along just fine without you. I don't know why I counted on you in the first place."

"That's a pretty rotten thing to say. I'm a very responsible husband and father. You've got no right to question my motives."

"Well, I guess if I have to believe either your words or your behavior, I should count on what you DO rather than what you say, since the two are different a lot of the time."

"Fine."

"Fine."

✿✿✿

You Were Right. I Was Wrong. Now What?

I sit tonight in a hotel room in Herndon, Virginia. It is cold, not uncommon for a January night in this part of the country. I've been here three nights, putting off booting the computer and committing to this final discourse.

Writing this book has been a fantastic experience for me. I've taken two months off and devoted most every day to writing. To finish, I thought of so many topics about which I might scribe but came up measuring Empty on my Impact Meter. With that as my intro to this brief chapter, I ask the reader to consider every word written here carefully. This topic touches the very fiber of relationships. It is about the heartfelt message of people who are hurt. It is about the essence of living and working together. It is about the soul of a family's existence.

> *San Francisco airport. Japan airlines DC-8. 1967.*
> "JAL 1234, you are cleared to land."
> "Thank you, San Francisco. Flaps 30 percent. Throttles 60 percent. Gear down."

This exchange might have been how the conversation was proceeding between Captain Aso and the tower at San Francisco airport. Unfortunately, the landing was anything but routine. Captain Aso proceeded to land the DC-8 stretch jet along the shoreline of San Francisco harbor, in perfect compass alignment with the runway, which was one mile away. Miraculously, the plane came to rest perched on two oyster beds, and with the exception of some structural damage to the landing gear, the airplane and passengers were relatively unharmed. His landing was so smooth that many people did not realize they were in the water until they saw sailboats passing by their windows.

America went nuts. The National Transportation Safety

Board began their investigation and prepared for years of lengthy battles and testimony as to what went wrong. The three major television networks transferred reporters and equipment to San Francisco, and they even signed one-year leases on apartments for their staff as they prepared to provide news coverage of the investigation.

The first day of testimony was a zoo. The investigators were seated behind their desks as they prepared to hear Captain Aso's version of the fiasco. Captain Aso strode confidently into the courtroom with his crew aligned behind him in order of seniority. Everyone was dressed in his best and most ornate uniform. The inquisition had begun.

The first question was, "Captain Aso, can you tell us, in your own words, please, how you managed to land that DC-8 stretch jet in San Francisco Harbor in perfect compass alignment with the runway?"

Captain Aso, a product of splendid Japanese heritage, understood the concept of apology and grace as it had been taught to him throughout his childhood. His response was (and I paraphrase for those with sensitive eyes), *"As you Americans say, Aso screwed up."*

For all intents and purposes, that was the end of the hearing. No one in authority actually considered that the senior pilot from Japan Airlines would admit fault. It was such a novel idea that one of the investigators actually missed it, returning late from a trip to the restroom as testimony had just begun.

In Japan, there is an ancient ceremony of Wa, which allows a person to admit fault, apologize for causing discomfort and trouble, and ask for grace. Grace can be defined as unwarranted and undeserved forgiveness. When the ceremony of Wa is complete, all parties invoke "intentional forgetfulness," and the infraction is never mentioned again.

The idea of grace is readily accepted in Japanese culture, churches and synagogues, and recovery organizations. Why it is ignored in business is befuddling.

It seems that when people are granted authority in organizations, they forget that their behaviors and decisions might adversely affect others who report to them. Most employees truly approach their jobs with the best of intentions. I know very few people who walk in the door on Monday morning thinking of new ways to screw around with the company or the people with whom they work.

Unfortunately however when things go wrong, apology is considered weakness by many. *Explanation* reigns supreme, regardless of the consequences experienced by those who were wronged. I firmly believe that all people in every organization should not only admit their errors when committed but should also sincerely apologize to those who they have hurt when committing those errors.

I spoke with a man a few months ago who was sobbing about his wife's behavior. He is a retired oil company executive, and worth millions. He's respected in the community and seen as a role model to many. He is *not* a wimp.

He and his wife had been married for more than forty years, and for only the second time in four decades, she apologized for something she had done. Her apology was two words long. She said, "I'm sorry."

The man was silently weeping *not* because of what she'd done or even because she had rarely apologized to him for anything that happened in the relationship. He was heartbroken because he realized how one-sided their relationship had been, and he felt how empty her apology seemed to him.

An apology is not about what you have done wrong as much

as it is about how the other person has been aggrieved. There are three steps to offering regret for your actions, effectively.

While the very fiber of our existence is contained within our personal DNA. I use these three letters to remind myself that admission of fault should also be part of me.

D — **Describe** exactly what you did wrong

N — **Needs** of the person to whom you are apologizing

A — **Ask** for forgiveness

Describe

When you describe what you have done wrong, *do not* attempt to justify why you did it. An apology is not about explaining your logic. Although an excepted apology goes a long way to making *you* feel better about the relationship, your burden is not to bolster *your* feelings but to repair the feelings of someone else. Too many apologies begin with a detailed explanation of how someone was really right in her behavior if only circumstances had occurred as she had planned or if people had behaved as they were supposed to behave. For an apology to be meaningful and accepted, these things are irrelevant.

When you describe what you did, stick to the facts. Admit to the errors in fact or judgment you made, and outline the results that happened as a result of your actions. *Do not* try to justify your actions. And don't try to sugar-coat them. Simply and succinctly state them.

Needs

The needs of the person whom you have wronged are paramount. Your actions are inconsequential at this point in the relationship. You have hurt someone. Acknowledge his disillusionment.

Begin with a statement like, *"If that were done to me, I would have felt. . . ."*

Reflect their emotions and responses as if what you had

done were indeed inflicted upon you. You must put yourself in their position to do this. You *cannot* do this from where you are but must instead do it from where *they* are.

Acknowledge their actions as well. If they have lashed out, complained, moaned, groaned, or become aggressive, you *must* validate their reaction with your own version of how *you* would have reacted if it were done to you. The word *empathize* is over-used when discussing supportive behavior, but here, it fits. Put yourself in their place.

An apology without changed behavior is essentially worthless. Abused spouses hear numerous apologies only to experience repeated behavior. A primal need of someone who has been wronged is validation of their feelings *and* assured change in future behavior.

Oftentimes, one's behavior causes hurt not because of what was done, but instead, how someone has been treated. Rushing out of a restaurant without waiting on your spouse to finish should merit an apology for behavior, but respect is probably the larger issue. The need here for changed behavior is not limited to restaurants, but probably to numerous aspects of the relationship where respectful behavior is not practiced.

When you acknowledge a person's feelings while apologizing, be sure *all* their needs are addressed. This might require a radical shift in not only how you act with, but also how you think of this person. The needs of someone who has been hurt are often camouflaged as powerlessness. The power you give through apology is dwarfed by the restored power with which the receiver is bestowed.

Ask Forgiveness

The apology transaction is two-sided. It takes only one side to apologize. It takes both sides to reconcile.

Intentional forgetfulness is the job of the person who was

hurt. Do *not push*. Often, the pain you have inflicted goes deeper than mere words on your part can repair. Reconciliation will take time. Depending on the depth of the pain, it could take from minutes to years.

Forgive and forget is an anomaly. Forgetting a wrong is nearly impossible. Being hurt, however, is not impossible to diminish, but it is difficult because the emotions of being wronged by someone is the root of pain in relationships. In time, with apology, the emotional turmoil of being wronged can be tempered.

Almost two years ago, I wrote an e-mail letter that was a scathing assessment of someone's perceived incompetence. I misdirected the e-mail addresses, sent it to the "world" within the company for which I was working, and consequently hurt the person about whom I was writing.

About an hour after I sent the e-mail, I realized my error in judgment and tried to "unsend" the message. I was too late, of course. Her response was to fight back. She called a senior person in the company demanding I be relieved of my responsibilities.

My apology to this woman was heartfelt. I realized I was operating outside of my values by writing the letter in the first place. It was wrong, and I had committed a grievous error in sending it at all. I apologized.

My letters, phone calls, visits, and e-mail messages went unanswered. To my grave will I take this event. How much sleep I lost and how much my blood pressure was raised are inconsequential compared to how wrong I was by writing that letter.

Some apologies will never be accepted, and reconciliation will sometimes never be realized. When these events occur, it is time to move on—but only after you've done *everything* you can think of to make things right.

Saying "I'm Sorry" doesn't get it if you can also send flowers. Being humble doesn't cut it when you can also mail a card. Face-to-face apologies might also not suffice if admitting fault to a parent or boss might also smooth things over.

Captain Aso had it figured out. He admitted fault, asked forgiveness, and moved on with his life. When you've done something hurtful to someone else, climb down from your perch and do the same thing Aso did. Even anonymous recovery groups have this down pat. Their twelve step programs include making a list and making amends to the people whom you have hurt by your past behavior. To the group members, it is a way of inducing closure to a past lifestyle as they prepare for a future that is much brighter. I think this method is a delightful way to close a chapter on a previous existence.

When you apologize, trust can be re-established. I define trust in this way:

I trust you when *your* behaviors support *my* values.

This rebirth of trust takes time. It also takes apology when the relationship has been breached. Trust is at the essence of being human.

Trust in ethical behavior is my number one value. When someone demonstrates ethical behavior repeatedly over time, I begin the process of trusting her.

When you've done something to hurt someone else, you've violated the "trust" factor. Time, apology, and renewed trustful behavior are the keys to repairing that infraction.

To trust other people is to bare your soul to them. I've met tens of thousands of people in my travels, and I count many of them as acquaintances or friends. Many of them are close friends who share my values and ambitions. I have only a few people on the planet, however, with whom I entrust my innermost thoughts.

Some people will think this is a small group of people with whom I can really "let my hair down." I believe it represents a vast multitude. The relationships I share with them are based on trust, respect, and love. In the course of our time together, I have hurt them at some time in our relationship. Some of them have hurt me too. Our apologies to each other and the shared values we live and demonstrate every day have made our continued friendships possible.

Count your heartfelt friends *carefully* right now. If you run out of fingers on one hand before you run out of names, you have lived a fortunate life. Nurture those relationships with love, laughter, and when necessary, apology.

APPENDIX

Ray's Reading List

Throughout our lives, we shape our intellect, ideas, values, and opinions. Most of this crafting comes from our environment. I've read many books and gleaned many ideas from people so much more learned than I. Scores have been responsible for planting the seeds of thought that eventually grew into this book. Some of their works are listed for your edification and study. I wish I could list them all.

Ken Blanchard has written dozens of books that teach simple yet timeless lessons of life and business. His first, *The One Minute Manager* was followed by *Leadership and the One Minute Manager*, which is the foundation for Situational Leadership® II, written as a parable. Written with Sheldon Bowles, *Gung Ho* is a Chinese term meaning "working together." It is an excellent read, and one of the best he has written. I recommend all of Ken's books, not because of our relationship, but because of the wisdom embedded in them, which I can to attest firsthand. You can also learn about walking your "faith" in *"Leadership by the Book"* and encouragement in *"Whale Done."*

Walk the Talk, Eric Harvey and Alexander Lucia, Performance Publishing, 1995

You Can Negotiate Anything, Herb Cohen, Carol Publishing Group, 1996

Soar With Your Strengths, and Now Break All the Rules, Donald O. Clifton and Paula Nelson, Dell, 1992

People Smart, Tony Alessandra and Michael J O'Connor, Keynote, 1990

How to Recognize and Reward Employees, Donna Deeprose, AMA, 1994

Type Talk and *Type Talk at Work,* Otto Kroeger and Janet Thuesen, Dell, 1992

Managing from the Heart, Hyler Bracey, Dell, 1990

Leading with Soul, Lee Bolman and Terrence Deal, Jossey-Bass, 1994

The Trust Factor, John O. Whitney, McGraw-Hill, 1994

1001 Ways to Reward Employees, Bob Nelson, Workman Publishing, 1994

Parenting with Love and Logic, Jim Fay and Foster Cline, Nav Press, 1990

The Customer Comes Second, Hal F. Rosenbluth, Quill, 1992

The Five Love Languages, Gary Chapman, Moody Press, 1996

The Five Dysfunctions of a Team, Patrick Lincioni, Jossi-Bass, 2002

The Holy Bible, One author, various writers, awesome wisdom, published worldwide. Try the New King James Version or the New International Version for easy-to-read and understandable translations.

This book has been "written" using computer software that recognizes my speech. Dragon Systems' "Naturally Speaking" is responsible for finally making the technology available to do so. Thank you, DragonSys, for giving this Extrovert the opportunity to SPEAK his thoughts and equipping my computer write them for me.

There are still four books in my mind just waiting to get out. They are *The Business of Marriage, The Business of Families for Dads, The Business of Families for Moms,* and *The Business of Families for Children.* I covet your input. Your stories and ideas will be cherished and accredited as I write them.

To learn more about Ray Snyder and future books, please visit his Web site at www.families.nu.

Send your stories, ideas, suggestions or comments via e-mail to ray@families.nu.

Ray A. Snyder is a native of Charleston, South Carolina. He graduated from The Baptist College at Charleston at the age of 20 and was commissioned as one of the youngest officers in the U. S. Air Force. Later, learning the business of training and development with Milliken and Company and the South Carolina State Ports Authority, he served as Senior Consulting Partner with The Ken Blanchard Companies® since 1989.

Ray earned his M.B.A. and an honorary Doctorate of Humanities from Charleston Southern University along the way. In 2004, he was named as one of the forty graduates of his alma mater who have made the most significant difference in the world. He has also been named as a Staley Distinguished Christian Scholar and is the Executive in Residence at CSU.

Ray's work with hundreds of the largest and most influential companies and government agencies in eight nations has made a difference in not only those organizations, but in the lives of tens of thousands of parents and children who have heard his message.

He has served with his family in Romania, working with volunteer missionaries to build an orphanage and mission center for homeless and hopeless Romanian children. His hundreds of stories have taught life lessons and values that translate perfectly in the language of a hungry and abused child.

At forty-eight years old, he exercised his "halftime," cutting his travel schedule of 120 days a year in half. His *new* career is a newfound passion to work with his wife, Kathy, as they fulfill their mission conducting marriage conferences that help families and specifically husbands and wives strengthen their relationships with each other, their families, and God. He is also working with young college students building Christian leaders who build Kingdom Companies after graduation.

Married since 1975, Ray and Kathy have raised two daughters: Megan and Mary Ann. Their extended family now includes Paul, Megan's husband, their "perfect in every way" granddaughter Lynn, Mickey, Mary Ann's husband, and Rufus, an adorable Berkeley (a little of all the dogs in Berkeley County) adopted from the pound in 2003.

www.ingramcontent.com/pod-product-compliance
Lightning Source LLC
Chambersburg PA
CBHW071354280526
45787CB00001B/321